Doing The Right Thing

A TEACHER SPEAKS

David Greene

Produced by:

FriesenPress

Suite 300 – 852 Fort Street

Victoria, BC, Canada V8W 1H8

www.friesenpress.com

Distributed to the trade by The Ingram Book Company

CONTENTS

PRAISE FOR DOING THE RIGHT THING

"I need a book like this to keep me going. David Greene describes, explains and persuades us that it's still possible to create great school experiences that matter. At long last, after a generation or two, we're hearing again from classroom teachers about what it means to stick to it and thus learn the job over the many year it takes. David Greene writes wonderfully about his discoveries in a way that both teaches and entertains. It will enlighten parents, teachers, and would-be policy makers."

- Deborah Meier- Deborah Meier on the board of the Coalition of Essential Schools and Mission Hill school, and the author of many books on her experiences. She was the first educator to receive a MacArthur Award, and is on the editorial board of The Nation, Dissent, and the Harvard Education Newsletter. She is a senior scholar at NYU.

"Dave Greene, one of the best teachers I have ever met, has written the most useful book about teaching I have read in the last ten years. Dave, who taught and coached at the Bronx's, Adlai Stevenson High School, before he moved to do the same at Woodlands and Scarsdale High Schools, has unparalleled experience as a program developer and teacher educator as well, having been involved in the WISE Program for high school seniors, and having mentored Teacher for America Corps members at Fordham University. When you add to this his role in founding the Save Our Schools movement, you can see what a depth of knowledge Dave can draw upon.

This book has incredible chapters on theories of pedagogy, what makes the best teachers effective, and how effective assessment is a logical outcome of the accumulated knowledge of our best teachers and administrators. Dave tears up the latest fashions in education reform, showing their unfortunate resemblance to Frederick Taylor's models of factory administration and has a brilliant critique of Teach For America's approach to teacher training and pedagogy based on his extensive experience working with TFA corps members in inner city schools.

You will come away from reading this book enraged at the powerful forces reshaping public education, but you will better understand what makes a better teacher. This my friends, is an unbeatable combination."

- Mark D Naison
Professor of African American Studies and History
Fordham University

———

"*Doing the Right Thing* is quite a collection of nimble, poignant proposals and stories that will strike a chord with educators, students, and parents. Pulsing with brilliance, David Greene carefully comments on the issues that will define the battles over school reform in America."

—Nikhil Goyal, Author of One Size Does Not Fit All: A Student's Assessment of School

———

"Dave Greene unravels education reform with the sharp eye of a lifelong educator. And from the threads of his own experiences he weaves a guide for anyone who wants to understand what makes a classroom work. Greene has worked in tough schools and knows what works. His experiences as a mentor for Teach For America corps members are revealing. School reform would look very different if we listened to real experts like Dave Greene."

- Anthony Cody, author, Living in Dialogue blog, Education Week/Teacher Magazine

———

"David Greene is an experienced educator who cares deeply about our children and the schools in which they learn. A fresh, reasoned perspective on education. This book is worth reading! "

-Peg Tyre, author of the Good School: how smart parents get their kids the education they deserve. (H.Holt. 2011)

———

"Dave Greene's book slams educational policy gone awry with boots-on-the-ground realism. He captures the reader from the onset with page-turning directness, gripping exemplars, clarity mixed with his unabashed writing style that holds nothing back, rich description and research, that blends data with his lifelong experiences in education. This book is a powerful read. Dave challenges the rhetoric on educational policy and debunks reform measures that tout testing, alternative pathways to the classroom, particularly, Teach For America, and a business model and comes off as a blend of investigative reporter, seasoned academic, and outraged citizen."

-Dr. Barbara Torre Veltri, Assistant Professor
Northern Arizona University
Recipient of 2011 Research and Creative Activity Award: "Most Significant Scholarly Work" from Northern Arizona University For the book: Learning on Other People's Kids: Becoming a Teach For America Teacher (Information Age Publishers, 2010).

———

David Greene | vii

"David Greene offers a brilliant and honest composite collection of the various issues emerging from corporate education reform's encroachment upon the teaching profession and our public education system; a composite which diverges where and when necessary to honor the complexities of teaching and learning, while holding together a central theme grounded in what matters most, as the prophetic first sentence in his first chapter states, "Let's start with kids." Greene deftly blends together theory and practice, past and present, problems and alternatives, research and wisdom, statistics with personal narrative, and humor and pain. The power of this book lies with its unflinching challenge to the rhetoric posed by corporate models of reform such as Teach For America, and charts a vision for change which we all must heed so that we do not, as Greene writes in his final closing words, "kiss our future goodbye."

> - **Morna McDermott McNulty. Associate Professor, College of Education Towson University**

————

"The so-called education reformers should read this book and find out what a REAL education reformer knows. Dave Greene has laid out a prescription for reforming our education system using tried and true values of supporting and respecting teachers and the teaching profession. His passions for teaching and extensive classroom experience are in abundant display here. Teachers will find this book to be a breath of fresh air because here is someone who really understands them and knows how to make their classrooms exciting places for children to grown and learn."

> - **Gary Axelbank. Host of *BronxTalk*, the Bronx' flagship TV talk show**

DEDICATION:

To:

Beatrice Greene, my mother, who always knew I would be a teacher...

Dr. Rita Stafford Dunn: I am the seed you planted in the 2nd grade in PS 66 Bx.

Phyllis Opochinsky, the best cooperating teacher a student teacher could ever hope to have.

My colleagues from Stevenson, Woodlands, and Scarsdale High Schools from whom I learned, and with whom I shared, the art and science of teaching.

ACKNOWLEDGEMENTS:

This book would not have been done without the encouragement of the most important people in my life, my wife, Jamie, my daughter, Lindsay, and my son, Ben. They always told me I should share my thoughts, ideas, and experiences with others, perhaps to give them some peace and quiet. I am glad they did.

After I finally graduated (ok, most would call it retired) I mentored several Teach For American corps members for whom I wrote short essays filled with advice. A few of them said I should put those together into a book. I told them I would if they stayed in teaching. Half did, so I started writing.

I must give a big shout out to Professor Mark Naison of Fordham University (AKA the Notorious Ph. D) who helped me figure out what I needed to add to make this (I hope) more than a boring tome on teaching. I guess I did ok. His foreword and cover quote humble me.

Finally I have to thank Madalyn Stone and Katharine Sands, two writing and publishing professionals who helped me fine tune, over and over again. Again.

FOREWORD

IN DEFENSE OF PUBLIC SCHOOL TEACHERS

There are few jobs in this country more challenging than that of a public school teacher. In a country with one of the highest rates of poverty in the industrialized world, with almost no social safety net to help struggling families, our teachers have to create a positive learning atmosphere in classrooms filled with young people under stress. The teacher not only has to be someone who can transmit knowledge and skills, he or she has to be a diplomat, a counselor, a surrogate parent, and occasionally a police officer. And those skills don't just extend to the students. The parents and caretakers (because many working-class and poor children live with grandparents or foster parents) are a challenge all by themselves, as many of them are under extreme stress and act out as almost as much as their children. And then there are the local school boards, and state authorities, who are putting teachers under pressure to have their students pass standardized tests and are looking to discipline them and fire teachers if they do not produce the desired results. A teacher today faces a complex variety of tasks that few people confront on their jobs--tasks that require intellect, creativity, patience, and imagination, and if all those fail, sheer stubbornness and courage.

You would think, given the difficulty of the task that teachers confront--the incredibly long hours they spend preparing lessons and grading assignments, as well as the tremendous time and expense they put into decorating their classrooms--that teachers would be revered and respected by the American public. But, in fact, the opposite is true.

Americans--more than any people in the world--seem to resent and even hate teachers!

How else to explain the propensity of people on all sides of the political spectrum who blame teachers for the persistence of poverty in the United States, for the failure of the United States to be economically competitive with other nations, and for disappointing test scores and graduation rates among racial minorities? We have the spectacle of the president of the United States praising the mass firing of teachers in a working-class town in Rhode Island where test scores were low; a school chancellor in the nation's largest city demanding the publication of confidential--and often misleading--teacher-rating data in the press; and a mass-market film about the power of teachers, which focuses exclusively on privately funded charter schools, conveniently leaving out the thousands of dedicated, often brilliant, public school teachers working in the nation's high-poverty districts.

As the child of two New York City public school teachers who each spent more than thirty years in the system, and as someone who spends a good deal of time interacting with teachers in Bronx schools through a community history project I direct, I find this hostility to teachers totally misguided. I invite anyone who thinks teachers are to blame for poverty and inequality to come with me on some of my trips to Bronx public schools and see the extraordinary efforts teachers and principals make to create learning environments for children that are filled with excitement and stimulation--even beauty. Look at the way classrooms and hallways are decorated. See the incredible projects teachers do with their students. See the plays and musical performances that the schools put on. And talk to the teachers and principals about what their students are up against. I will never forget the closed-door meeting I had with a Bronx principal-- whose school served three meals a day--where he described how many of his children started crying on Friday because they were afraid they wouldn't eat until they came back to school on Monday. Or talk to a teacher who is working in a class where half the students don't live with their biological parents, and get a sense of the desperate need these children have for love and affection.

I would like to see how well Secretary of Education Arne Duncan or New York City Schools Chancellor Dennis Walcott would do prepping students for tests if they taught in a Bronx middle school or high school where half the students are on the verge of dropping out because of family pressures or problems reading and writing in English. The teachers who come to these schools and give students love as well as instruction are not cynically collecting their paychecks; they are taking responsibility for all the problems our society has neglected and for the family and community services it fails to provide.

In a society without adequate day care, health care, and recreation for working-class families, where people have to work two or three jobs to stay in their apartments or share those apartments with multiple strangers; where young people face violence and stress in their living quarters, as well as on the streets; where sports and music programs are only available for those who can pay; our public school teachers have one of the hardest jobs in society.

They deserve respect and support, not contempt. They are among America's true heroes.

Mark D. Naison

Chair of African and African-American Studies

Fordham University

Bronx, NY

Founder and principal investigator of the Bronx
African-American History Project

October 25, 2010

PREFACE

Concerned parents all across the country are asking: What's wrong with our public schools? What's wrong with our teachers? All parents are right to ask these questions. The problems are immense. The solutions are complex. There is much to be fixed. Students of all ages are not challenged. They are bored. They are being tested to death. The love of learning is instilled in far too few students of all socioeconomic backgrounds. Policy makers do not listen to parents, teachers, and students.

Additionally there are simply not enough good teachers to go around. All of our kids deserve the kind of teachers we had that inspired us to learn, to grow, to become better students and human beings. How do we get them? Why are there so few inspiring teachers? What about our system prevents it? What about the new reforms make it worse, not better? We all deserve answers.

For us to continue to be the democracy we care for, we must provide for a better-educated electorate. To accomplish that we must fix our schools, fix our curricula, fix how we recruit our teachers and, finally fix how our teachers are taught to teach so they can be most effective in today's world.

However there is much already very good about our schools. There are excellent schools with excellent teachers in excellent districts all around the country. There are programs and styles to be shared. But who knows of those? If you are lucky enough to live in one of them you know. But if you don't, what information do you rely on to judge American schools and teaches? Who are your sources?

Our nation's media, conservative and liberal alike spread misinformation. They vilify the teaching profession, regardless of how successful many teachers are with children of all ages. Our politicians implement laws and plans based on that misinformation. Foundations are giving huge sums of money based on that misinformation. Corporations are profiting from that misinformation.

We need real information. There are millions of student and parent voices crying out to be heard. There are thousands of well-informed academics and educational leaders who cry out but simply are out spent by the misleaders. Finally, there are thousands of smart, caring, engaging, and inspiring teachers who must be heard. I am but one teacher trying to make a difference. The public must be made more aware of the truth about American education today before it is too late.

This book started as a series of tips for the several TFA Corps members I mentored between 2008 and 2012 while I worked for Fordham University. Over time it morphed into a series of essays on teaching and issues facing education and finally it has become this attempt to inform the public of what schools can become and teachers should be doing in the best interests of our children.

The problem worsens as I write. Just this past week Chicago closed 54 schools. According to National Public Radio, at least 10 cities have filed complaints with the Education Department's Office of Civil Rights since January. Another 33 complaints in 22 states are pending, but there's no indication that school closings will stop anytime soon. I cannot keep up. We must put a halt to the destruction of public education.

WHY I AM?

I am a teacher. I am a parent. I am a mentor. I am a coach. I taught, advised, coordinated, and coached in three high schools in New York City and Westchester for over thirty-eight years. Since 2008, I have been trying to pass on what I was taught and what I learned through my various experiences to new teachers.

In 2009 I was told by my boss at a local, highly respected school of education that I was doing too much for the first-year Teach For America (TFA) corps members with whom I worked. Beware, those who never heard of TFA. Here is its brief story. In 1990, a charter corps of 500 committed recent college graduates became Teach For America and attempted to fill the teacher gap in poor schools around the nation. It was supposed to be a Peace Corps for American Education. Lots of people were excited by that prospect, even me. But 23 years later it has become one tentacle of the power-grabbing octopus attempting to privatize pubic education. More on that later.

I was told that I should just visit and talk with them. I shouldn't send them samples of good pedagogy; I shouldn't keep a running journal with them to keep a record of observations and discussions; I shouldn't burden them because they have a TFA mentor and maybe a school mentor and certainly an instructor from the university. It turned out, most didn't.

A lot has happened since I last thought I finished writing this book. First, I am no longer working at that highly respected university. A number of factors explain this occurrence. It is facing budget issues. The number of traditional, graduate education students is shrinking--especially in my area of expertise, social studies--because of several factors. Simply stated, there are just fewer job opportunities, even with early retirements, as public schools shrink or are closed and replaced by charter schools that seem to want to hire nontraditionally trained teachers. Teach for America (TFA) no longer sends it social studies or English candidates. It encourages its teaching candidates, traditional or TFA, to become certified as special education teachers, as well as in their subject specialty, to give these young folks a greater opportunity to be hired. When my boss told me that the only work available for me was to supervise new, special education TFA Corps Members, I said I couldn't. I was not licensed or qualified in that very specific area. When I asked if there were any other opportunities, the answer was no.

There may also be another explanation, as some of my more paranoid friends and colleagues think. I was a gadfly. I made a lot of noise nationally about TFA and how it adversely affected teaching as a profession. I made noise about the new rubric system being used to evaluate my mentees. Was I let go because of that? I hope not.

As a result of this loss of employment and my recent resignation from coaching football, I now have more time to devote to my beloved Wise Individualized Senior Experience (WISE) program (www.wiseservices. org) and to my work on the national scene, trying to fight the powers of devastating reform. I am now the Treasurer of Save Our Schools National (SOS). SOS is an organization in support of all public school students, parents, and teachers. We are against high-stakes testing and corporate control of the public school systems (www.saveourschoolsmarch.org).

In August of 2011, I gave two workshops at the first SOS march and conference in Washington, DC. One was on how to reinvigorate the American high school, and the other was on the hype of Teach For America. At Occupy DOE DC in the spring of 2012, I gave another talk on TFA. Perhaps the paranoids were right? I spoke again at Occupy DOE DC 2 the weekend of April 4-7, 2013 with a new colleague, then 18 year-old Nikhil Goyal, on how to reinvent the American high school. Nikhil is the author of a highly praised book on education entitled *One Size Does Not Fit All*. He is a recent graduate from Syosset High School in NY. He introduced me to Josh Lafazan, also of Syosset, New York, who is the youngest elected member of a New York State school board. It is quite fascinating to see such bright, young men totally engaged in the work of making schools better for students.

What's been going on most recently in the fight for public education? The election of Barack Obama was supposed to bring a sigh of relief to embattled, public educators. Instead, it brought more heartache and disappointment. The new Secretary of Education, Arne Duncan (not an educator) put into effect a "replacement" for No Child Left Behind (NCLB) that turned out to be no such thing. State governments jumped at the chance to get out from under NCLB's impossible mandate of having all children be reading proficient by 2014. They jumped at the bribe of more federal money. The catch was that they had to follow the new guidelines of the replacement—The Race to the Top (RTTT). Which state was going to be the best state in the Union? But at what cost?

By accepting RTTT, states would now be forced to give more standardized tests; collect more scientifically based data (that has shown that these new techniques that are forced down public educators' throats do not work); evaluate teachers using this data; follow a "Common Core" of standards that will use even more tests; privatize more schools and districts; force more good teachers out of teaching; hire more noncertified teachers from programs like TFA; pay even less regard to the professional expertise of teaching professionals; and worse, pay even less attention to how children learn best.

The evidence of the resulting crumbling of public education all over the country is overwhelming. Instead of "getting rid of bad teachers," more good and excellent teachers are leaving. Teaching colleagues, who three years ago said they loved their job and would stay until someone carried them out, are now saying they can't wait until they are eligible for retirement. Whereas, in 1990, the average length of a teaching career was approximately fifteen years, it is now five. School districts all over the country, hit hard by the repercussions of the Great Recession and increased costs of all the new testing and mandates (of course, underfunded by the bribe), are now looking for ways to cut their budgets. They have cut courses, recess, and gym. They have limited electives and extracurricular activities. They have closed schools and eliminated teaching positions. Even more diabolically, many more have figured out a way to use these new rules to force more expensive, credentialed teachers out and replace them with short-timers not lasting more than two to five years. As a result, more districts and states are lowering labor costs and limiting future pension costs. The bottom line wins. Teachers? No! Students? No! Parents? No!

Examples abound. The crisis is deepening. However, there is hope that we have turned the corner. More and more grassroots organizations, (like SOS, Journey for Justice, and United Opt–Out National, and Support the Garfield High School MAP Boycott), are being organized and fighting back. Social networking and Facebook pages have allowed people in support of public education to reach out and help each other. Teacher organizations, not just unions, are fighting back. Administrator organizations are fighting back. Parent organizations are fighting back. Student organizations are fighting back. Even school boards are fighting back—if they have overcome their fears.

As Franklin Delano Roosevelt said so many years ago: "All we have to fear is...fear itself." As the great civil rights song title says: "We Shall Overcome." Today's fight for public education is today's civil rights fight. We must stop fearing the loss of federal monies. I cringe when I say this, but there was one thing Rick Perry might have been right about in his famous 2012 debate meltdown. Maybe we should eliminate the Department Of Education (DOE) if it doesn't listen to its experts in the field and its clients.

Most importantly, we have to stop listening to the hype about how bad public education in this country is compared to other counties. There are plenty of things to change. We need to make learning and teaching as fun as it once was in kindergarten. Most of all, it cannot be one size fits all. It has to account for students' individual learning styles. It must use technology advantageously. It must improve teachers' preparation and continued growth as professionals. It needs to look at how countries like Finland turned their systems around by doing many of the things we did forty years ago in public education and taking care of the whole child from an early age. For a wonderful description of this process and how Finland became so successful in public education, I strongly suggest reading Pasi Sahlberg's *Finnish Lessons: What Can the World Learn from Educational Change in Finland.* When we are compared to the world's top nations using international tests like the Program for International Student Assessment (PISA), we rank 17th in various subjects like reading, math, and science. Finland ranks 3rd. However, Finland has a poverty rate of 4 percent, while approximately 22 percent of US children live in poverty. We simply refuse to face that fact. When poverty is taken out of the equation, the US would rank in the top five.

PISA recognizes the important effects of socioeconomic conditions on education:

> Home background influences educational success, and schooling often appears to reinforce its effects... the socioeconomic background of students and schools does appear to have a powerful influence on performance. Regardless of their own socioeconomic background, students attending schools with a socioeconomically advantaged intake tend to perform better than those attending schools with more disadvantaged peers. (http://www.oecd.org/pisa/pis aproducts/46619703.pdf)

One last point. Adversarial relationships are also ruining public education. The most successful school districts have collegial agreements about teaching, curriculum design, and working conditions jointly resolved through a strong tie between administrators, parent groups, policy makers, and teacher collective–bargaining organizations, whether called unions or associations. The least successful districts seem to have far more adversarial relationships, or there is an attempt by those in power to destroy those organizations to save labor costs, regardless of the unintended consequences. What are they thinking?

Recently, I was at my doctor's office getting a physical. We were talking about his group's new offices and whether or not they would be permanent. He said, "Doctors doing real estate...oy vey, who knows?" He then went on to discuss how doctors, lawyers, and businessmen are often those who think that because they are good at what they do, they can be good at telling others how to do their work. Of course, I chuckled. It sounded very familiar.

He told me that the best patients he has are teachers, because no matter how brilliant they are, they know their limitations and would not dare tell a doctor how to perform surgery. Again, I chuckled. But this time I told him how education is exactly like his example of doctors in real estate. It was the abridged version, as he was taking my blood pressure at the time.

We finally discussed how his role as a doctor is more and more being dictated by the drug and insurance company "medical experts" is exactly like how our roles as teachers are more and more being dictated by corporate "education experts"—in both cases for huge profits. Then I recruited him to join SOS.

CHAPTER 1:
_____

WHAT STUDENTS NEED

RESPECT AND SCHOOL CULTURE

Let's start with kids. For them, respect is as important as motivation, often more so. I am not talking about their respect for teachers. They respect those who respect them. Don't get me wrong. They want structure and authority. But they need to know that their teachers understand their "code of the street", wherever that street is, as much as teachers need to reinforce the code of the school. As Elijah Anderson wrote in *Code of the Street* (1999), "Respect becomes critical....Much of the code has to do with achieving and holding respect. And children learn its rules early." That respect is from their peers, who they have to live with outside of your class and the school. "The street serves as a mediating influence under which children may have to reconsider and rearrange their personal orientations....Adolescents everywhere are insecure and trying to establish their identities....In poor, inner-city neighborhoods, verbal prowess is important for establishing identity...the need for being in physical control of at least one portion of one's environment becomes internalized."

In the streets and in schools, Anderson asserts that, "even small children test one another, pushing and shoving...ready to hit other children over matters not to their liking." Why? To maintain respect. "By the fourth grade, enough children have opted for the code of the street that it begins to compete effectively with the culture of the school, and the code begins to dominate their public culture—in the school as well as out.... In one elementary school, I learned from interviewing kindergarten, first grade-, second grade-, and fourth-grade teachers that through the first grade about a fifth of the students were invested in the code of the street; the rest are interested in the subject matter and eager to take instruction from the teachers—in effect, well disciplined. By the fourth grade, though, about three-quarters of the students have bought into the street or oppositional culture." In this social setting, decent kids learn how to 'code switch' because...for many alienated young black people, attending school and doing well becomes negatively associated with acting white."

Anderson also states, "Education is thus undermined because the mission of the school *cannot* equal the mission of the kids.... Alienated students take on the oppositional role so effectively that they often become role models for other kids," thus gaining more respect. And in this environment, respect is necessary for getting along. Even "good kids" gain points for "going bad." "This coming of age process has implications for relations with...teachers." A formerly good student may stop doing homework, disobey, argue, talk back, and become more of an adversary.

So, here is where teachers come in! How do they change that? How do they explain the value of the school culture? How do they inspire and motivate kids to go against the grain and maintain their place in their world, while learning the ropes of ours?

One thing teachers have to do is learn to be able to code switch. Where the school is located doesn't matter. "You have to be tough. If you show fear, others will exploit it." Too often, though, teachers unfortunately mistake authoritarianism for toughness (as do obnoxious cops and administrators) and thus fail to "respect to be respected." In that case, kids, even young ones, will take on an oppositional role, and you will have done nothing but add fuel to the fire. A teacher that shows fear is done. "Put a fork in her." Show fear, and you are vulnerable to being undone.

Personally, I learned this from day one of my teaching profession. From the time I started at Adlai Stevenson High School, the staff was encouraged to become part of the fabric of our kids' lives by getting involved in extracurricular activities and coaching. At Stevenson, I was senior class advisor, an associate dean of discipline, an assistant varsity football coach, and a baseball coach. Many of us chaperoned dances and concerts and other evening activities, even dressing up at Halloween. We helped them with their class plays.

We also helped students through panic attacks in the middle of the night. We talked them through breakups and make-ups with girlfriends and boyfriends. We helped them navigate some damn rough waters. We tried to thwart suicide. We became part of their lives and their community. Forty-plus years later, many of us still are. We meet for reunions, dinners, and parties. We are Facebook friends. That kind of atmosphere is where teachers can do their best work.

TEACHERS NEED RESPECT TOO

In two of the three schools I worked, I was hired as a result of a collaborative effort between members of the social studies department, its department chairperson, and the principal. The principal--as opposed to over 95 percent of principals across the nation--simply heeds the advice of the particular department committee. The superintendent, in almost all cases, approves. It is the way hiring is done there. Over the twenty-two years I worked in these two schools, I was part of hiring committees for new members for my departments and new department chairs. Principals and assistant principals were hired using the same procedure. Another way these schools made new teachers comfortable, regardless of previous years of experience, was by giving them a mentor-teacher from within their own department. As I keep saying, rational models for "reform" are readily available. The Scarsdale School District, as an example, (through teamwork between union and management) has tackled some of the issues regarding teacher evaluation, hiring, and firing.

Moreover, all teachers are encouraged to seek out professional development in addition to that provided by the district. The district's union, the Scarsdale Teacher's Association, has run and continues to run a hugely successful teachers institute for the very purpose of teacher professional development, in addition to the ability to move up the pay scale this training provides. It is a worthwhile incentive. Financial incentives are used in business, why not in education?

These are the norms in one of the most prestigious school districts in the nation and the world. Does it have to provide all of this for teachers? Do the union and board have to collaborate in making these issues contractual in a district filled with high achievers and motivated wealthy students? Do they have to keep class sizes smaller and give teachers office hours, rather than hall and lunch duties? Probably not, but they know these approaches help their students achieve even more. They also know that these conditions, as well as providing high salaries and good benefits, attract the most professional teachers the nation has to offer.

Working in a place where excellence, hard work, and creativity are rewarded in many ways is continuous motivation. I have seen what happens when that atmosphere does not exist. Surrounded by good teachers who were not afraid to share ideas, better teaching transpired. We worked together to improve each other and ourselves. Teachers at Scarsdale, more so than administrators, pushed for new technology, new techniques, better, more authentic assessments.

Unfortunately, in the name of "reform," that atmosphere is being taken away in some schools. The following letter received by Professor Mark Naison of Fordham University from a former student describes what might occur to many schools in the near future:

> As a former student in your classes at Fordham, I remember the passion in your teaching. As a high school teacher, I believe I...bring passion to my work. I work in a school that was founded on teacher autonomy and governance. With this structure comes responsibility and creativity. However, with all the new rating systems and assessments, the director is finding it more difficult each day to preserve the structure we have built and thrive in. More pressure is being placed on all of us to perform in prescribed ways--a pressure that is felt by teachers and students alike. We are an extremely successful school or were an extremely successful school measured by our graduation rate, attendance, and portfolio assessment panels. This will change as more standardized assessments are forced upon us. Again, fortunately I am at a school that values teacher autonomy and creativity. I am more concerned about schools (usually in poorer areas of the city) that do not have the history, leadership, or

political base to question and to buffer the impact of
these new 'empirically tested' curricula and assessments.
It is a hard battle we need to fight.

Yes we do. And we better fight hard. We also have to pay what we learned forward. My life and career is the result of paying it forward. I was the product of what was passed on to me over the years. I passed on whatever wisdom I acquired over the years to students, to student teachers, to first-year teachers I mentored, to colleagues, to my kids. Retired from teaching, I have not retired from paying it forward. If more of us don't do this, the school culture teachers and students require will be lost.

When I taught in the Bronx, at the now-defunct Adlai Stevenson High School, we taught the same population that exists there today. However, many of us--young, enthusiastic, and well-trained by our mentors--were given the academic respect and motivation to help each kid, no matter his or her ability, reach for the highest standards of excellence. We often succeeded. We graduated countless numbers of college grads and professionals, as well as skilled, non-college professionals and workers. Of course, we failed, too--but not for lack of trying.

CLASS CULTURE

If the school you work in or your child goes to doesn't help teachers maintain what many authors and experts have identified as the five aspects of classroom culture, you are dead meat. They are Discipline, Engagement, Control, Influence, and Management (D.E.C.I.M.) Often misinterpreted, these five principles are the keys to a successful school and its classrooms. Not only is it necessary to accurately define these principles; it is even more necessary to use them *naturally*. The order these are presented is not relevant. They are like the five fingers on a hand. Each does its own thing, but together they make a powerful fist.

Discipline: This is a misused word. Think not of disciplining students. Think of their self-discipline. Do they have the self-discipline to do the right thing, the right way, for the right reasons? Do they have the self-control? Do they have the focus to follow the instructions? Can they understand the process? Do they know how to be students? If students don't, they have to be taught. Who else, but the classroom teacher will teach them how to be a successful student and class member? We cannot assume they already know. Most kids, even those exhibiting the most street culture traits, want to do well. They want to live up to high expectations given by someone they believe believes in them. However, as much as they might want to, they may not have a clue as to how to live up to those expectations. Sometimes, this even means teaching what may be mundane and obvious steps.

Engagement: This is a powerful word. Kids learn best while engaged in activities that inspire learning. They are what they do. The more they are positively and intrinsically engaged in learning, the sooner they believe in themselves as positively and intrinsically engaged learners. As this is internalized in more and more students, the classroom atmosphere is more conducive to learning without external manipulation. As Benjamin Franklin put it, "Tell me and I forget. Teach me and I remember. Involve me and I learn."

Control: The best, most powerful controllers are invisible. Advertisers control you. They get you to think you need something you never wanted in the first place. What supervisors call classroom management is really classroom control. It is power clearly, yet invisibly, wielded. Walk into a classroom where students are sitting up, actively participating without much prodding, listening to each other, and you are in a controlled environment. Their proper behaviors speak volumes. Ultimately, it is the specific, concise, positive, firm, encouraging, civil, respectful language of control that creates these classrooms.

Influence: Internalize. Inspire. Influence. Taken together, we have the kind of influence we want to have with our students. Internal drive (as Daniel Pink points out in his 2009 book, *Drive*) motivates best. When students know our belief in them is strong, they respond positively. Our best teachers were our most inspiring. They are the ones who influence us to go on to bigger and better things.

Management: Often, the first thing new teachers are told to concern themselves with is "classroom management." Too often, it is the only thing they are told to concern themselves with. How wrong is that? Management is a corporate word. It is a system of rewards and punishments to control and reinforce behavior. If we understand that, we see how wrong it is to focus on management to create a positive classroom culture. Do we want kids using extrinsic motivation (hope of reward, fear of punishment) to inspire learning? I don't think so. We have all seen those classrooms. Psychologists know extrinsic motivation simply changes what is important to kids. It changes the rules of the survival game. As a result of our new teaching dynamic, many teachers, being human and easily swayed by incentives, simply stop helping kids learn and instead ensure they do well on tests. These are not the same goals or achievements. Over time, the rewards and punishments have to escalate in order to have the same effects. Ultimately, the outcome is that students recognize the failure of teachers to motivate and believe in them. This is no way to have relationships with students, and, as we know, the ability to develop relationships makes good teachers better.

If these principles are used apart from each other, the sound of a classroom is a cacophony of random musical notes. Together, these five principles make a powerful song of learning. A classroom should dance to the music of D.E.C.I.M. As "Sly" Stewart of Sly and The Family Stone wrote in his song, "Dance to the Music":

> All we need is a drummer, **(Discipline)**
> For people who only need a beat, yeah!
>
> I'm gonna add a little guitar, **(Engagement)**
> And make it easy to move your feet.
>
> I'm gonna add some bottom, **(Control)**
> So that the dancers a-just won't hide.
>
> You might like to hear my organ, **(Influence)**
> I said, "Ride, Sally, Ride, now."
>
> If I could a-hear the horns blow, **(Management)**
> Cynthia on the throne, yeah!

Listen to the verses.
Dance to the Music. Oh!
Dance to the Music.
Dance to the Music.

Teachers who follow these five principles in their classrooms make beautiful music. Their kids dance the dance of learning. That is the way it is with great teaching. The culture created by that great teacher makes it work. It's like the air we breathe. We only really notice it when it is polluted.

WHAT DO YOU WANT FROM ME, PERFECTION?

No, but what do you want from yourself? Mediocrity? Twenty seven years ago, I had just left New York City after sixteen years of teaching and coaching and was in my first year teaching and coaching football in a high school noted for its good athletes, yet underachieving teams. It was quite apparent that no one had ever pushed these talented kids to do their "techniques" correctly. Experienced coaches (and teachers) will tell you that less gifted student athletes can do better than more gifted athletes with the proper techniques done the proper way, as close to 100 percent of the time as possible. It is what winners do.

This one day, I was working with the defensive linemen on stance and start drills, the football equivalent to the most basic reading or math skill, necessary for everything else to work properly. One of my charges (I'll call him Ray) was a big, fast kid who had been continually frustrated by players of lesser ability blocking him. On this day, one of his first with me, I kept making him do the drill over and over again, so that he would get it right each time on his own, without prodding. After having been told to do it again, after more times than he had ever been urged to do it, he turned to me and, in a frustrated voice, asked, "What do you want from me, perfection?" My answer was, "No, but what do you want from yourself? Mediocrity?" He paused a second, then went back to work. He eventually went on to be an all-league and semi-pro player at that position.

What he learned is what all students need to learn. They need to raise their bars higher. Regardless of the sets of standards "educrats" create, if we don't get our kids to raise the standards or goals they shoot for, they will forever be mediocre. Of course, we don't want these goals to be unobtainable, but they need to be high enough so that there is a challenge to meeting them. A by-product of these goals is that even if they aren't reached, they have surpassed the lesser goals they, or others, may have set.

All kids can learn. All kids can achieve. Can all be A students? No. Should they be? No. As in teaching and football playing, being a successful student is based partly on talent and partly on skill development. If SAT scores are the best indicator (of the standardized tests, that is) of success rates in college, the rich, white folks in Scarsdale know that, and their culture breeds success. However, too few of the poor Hispanic and Black folks in the Bronx can overcome the overwhelming street culture of the inner city. Our question should really be, how do we develop these kids' skills to match their talents, while fighting the influence of the street culture they are in? *It's the culture, stupid.* What do we do? Do we dumb down their curriculum and teach to minimal standards? Or, do we find it within oursleves to drive them to seek "perfection," rather than mediocrity?

Belief is contagious. Confidence is contagious. Enthusiasm is contagious. Passion is contagious. It is easy to spot a classroom where those qualities are part of the culture with the intrinsic motivation to achieve those goals. However, even with the most able and intrinsically motivated students, these classroom traits don't magically appear. Teachers make them happen. Teachers create a classroom where those are the expected states of mind. You know it. You know which teachers' classes you raced to because it was fun to learn there? Yes, learning can be fun. Students don't expect it, but are damn well more motivated and happy when it is fun. It is part of a teacher's job to make learning both serious and serious fun.

Why don't students expect classes like that? Remember most of your teachers? *No.* It was true then and it is true now. If the teacher doesn't make the class interesting, serious, and yet fun, what did your "less inhibited" classmates do, even if you grew up with well-behaved suburbanites? That's right, they became class clowns or made their own fun.

PASSION

Passion is an important yet often underused word. Don't we want our kids to feel passionate about what they do? Too often, the reason they don't is because they don't see us model it. Again, remember the zeal and zest your best teachers exhibited, and how that made you feel during their class. "Why is Mr. G. jumping on that desk to make that speech?" "Why is Ms. L. running around the room" rather than staying in front of the room like most teachers?

Good teachers make the classroom a place where humor is the norm. They make a room "ours," not just his or hers. They make it a place where everyone can safely be themselves. They make rooms where mutual respect is the norm. They make rooms where students are not afraid to try. They know it is ok to give a wrong answer, not because it will be accepted, but because it (not they) will be corrected without fanfare. It's just normal trial and error. If at first you don't succeed. . . .Develop more of those classrooms, and watch kids soar.

THE DEFAULT SETTING

Daniel Pink asks, "What is our default setting?" What infant or toddler isn't curious and self-directed? What happens to that child in middle and high school? He (more than she) has switched off to a passive, inert, and bored default. Who did that to us? What norms have socialized our default setting out of us? Have we, for the sake of scientific class management, made the loss of autonomy, curiosity, and self-directedness the opportunity cost of that decision?

In tomorrow's world, we need adults to think like intelligent adults, not programmed children. Those with only the skills produced by today's minimal standards and assessments will not have the techniques and tools they need to escape poverty, even working-class poverty. Often, reformers talk of preparing students to walk the path to college. The problem is today's reformers haven't walked in these students' shoes. We need to go further. Too many get to college and don't finish. According to Linda Darling-Hammond, Charles E. Ducommun Professor of Education,

Stanford University (education.nationaljournal.com, 9/15/09), "despite all of our investments in high school reform, only about 50 percent of ninth-graders enter postsecondary education, and only about 35 percent graduate with a college degree--about half the rate of countries like Finland and Korea that have been intensely reforming their education systems." Our students must be successful college graduates, not college dropouts.

Thomas Freidman, in *The World Is Flat*, poses the question of how to better prepare newer generations of Americans to succeed in the future as we face more rapid globalization. First, he quotes Princeton economist Alan Blinder who notes, "In the future, *how* we educate our children may prove to be more important than *how much* we educate them." That inspired Friedman to pose the following questions: "What is the "right education" young people need to prepare for the new middle [class], jobs, and how do we go about it?" He "discovered" four skill sets, none of them new.

1. **"Learn how to learn**--to constantly absorb, and *teach yourself* new ways of doing old things or new ways of doing new things."

2. **"Passion and curiosity"** -- Here he quotes Doc Searls, senior editor of the *Linux Journal* and noted technologist. "Of course, the average [student]...is still plentiful.... Most of them were made that way. They were shaped in large measure by school systems that have had, from the dawn of the industrial age, a main purpose: to produce employees for boxed positions.... *Work matters, but curiosity matters more. Nobody works harder than a curious kid."* Friedman, in fact, wants to "engrave that onto the door of every school in America." (Apparently no one in power read this.)

3. **"Plays well with others"**-- "Although having good people skills has always been an asset in the working world, it will be even more so in a flat world. That said, I am not sure how you teach that as part of a classroom curriculum, but someone had better figure it out." (Many great teachers have, Mr. Friedman.)

4. **"The right brain stuff"**--We need to nurture the right brain

more..."context, emotional expression, and synthesis." Again he asks, "But how exactly do you go about nurturing your right brain skills?" and he answers, "By doing something you love to do—or at least like to do—because you will bring something intangible to it, something out of your right brain, which cannot be easily repeated, automated, or outsourced." As Daniel Pink, author of *A Whole New Mind: Moving from the Information Age to the Conceptual Age*, explains, "The sorts of abilities that matter most now turn out are also the sorts of things that people do out of *intrinsic motivation*." Is this testing? *No*. It's good teaching.

Friedman tells us that a successful student is a "kid with a passion to learn and a curiosity to discover over a less passionate kid with a high IQ.... How do you create them? Through great teaching and opportunities to learn by making available to them all that is out there for their curiosity to digest." He states, "You need to discover your inner fire truck." Successful students from all walks of life can find their inner fire truck. However, many have never been given the opportunity. How can you, under even the most trying circumstances, accomplish what others have failed to do? Look forward to the challenge of giving kids "The Friedman Four."

INTRINSIC MOTIVATION

Learning is either algorithmic or heuristic (according to Daniel Pink, author of *Drive*, 2009). Algorithmic learning is done through a prescribed set of instructions driven toward a given conclusion, while heuristic learning is done through the creation of a solution to a problem. Today's world has seen a shift from jobs requiring algorithmic-style learning to those necessitating a more problem solving, heuristic one. That is not to say that today's students do not have to be skilled in both. Of course they do; we must teach both sets of skills. The education reforms led by NCLB, RTTT, and test prepping concentrate on only one, algorithmic learning, precisely the wrong skill set for the twenty-first century.

Together with a trend in education reform toward algorithmic style is the reward and punishment sanctioning that accompanies it.

Unfortunately, this is backward thinking. Of course, this "carrot and stick" approach works in algorithmic, boring, routine jobs. However, when introduced in more heuristic and interesting work, it has exactly the opposite effect. Rewards, as good as they sound, can turn interesting work into drudgery. They ruin creative and problem- solving performance because they remove intrinsic motivation. It is intrinsic motivation that is the key to success in non-algorithmic learning and tasks.

Researchers Edward Deci, Mark Lepper, Robert Nisbett, and David Greene (not me) discovered in 1973 that children who expected an extrinsic reward (contingent, if-then) lost interest in a task to a much greater extent than children who had no expectation of reward. They lost their intrinsic motivation and sense of autonomy. In fact, these findings were so startling that in 1999, Deci and two other researchers reanalyzed the data from 128 experiments and found "tangible rewards had a sub-stantially negative effect on intrinsic motivation," and institutions like schools cause considerable, long-term negative effects when they "focus on the short-term and opt for controlling people's behavior" (Pink 2009).

Teresa Amabile of the Harvard Business School replicated these find-ings in other studies. She and others found that contingently rewarded subjects have a harder time coming up with original solutions to problems or more creative responses to tasks. In another example, schoolchildren paid in some way to solve math problems typically choose easier prob-lems and actually earn less (Benabou and Tirole 2003).

A Thursday, April 8, 2010 *Time* article by Amanda Ripley, "Should Kids Be Bribed to Do Well in School?" examined this very issue. She stated,

> Teachers complain that we are rewarding kids for doing what they should be doing of their own volition. Psychologists warn that money can actually make kids perform worse by cheapening the act of learning. Parents predict widespread slacking after the incentives go away. And at least one think-tank scholar has denounced the strategy as racist. The debate has become a proxy battle for the larger war over why our kids are not learning at the rate they should be, despite decades of reforms and budget increases. But all this time, there has been only

one real question, particularly in America's lowest-performing schools: Does it work?

She examined the work of a Harvard economist named Roland Fryer Jr. in four cities: Chicago, Dallas, Washington, and New York.

In New York City, the $1.5 million paid to 8,320 kids for good test scores did not work. Fourth-graders could earn a maximum of $25 per test, and seventh-graders could earn up to $50 per test. The students were universally excited about the money, and they wanted to earn more. When researchers asked them how they could raise their scores, the kids mentioned test-taking strategies, like reading the questions more carefully. They did not talk about the substantive work strategies that lead to learning. In Chicago, Fryer worked with schools chief Arne Duncan, now President Obama's Education Secretary. Under a different model, the findings were mixed. Here, kids were paid for grades—a result they could not always control. Kids who got paid did indeed get better grades and attended class. These students did not, however, do better on their standardized tests.

In Washington, the kids did better on standardized reading tests. Getting paid on a routine basis for a series of small accomplishments, including attendance and behavior, seemed to lead to more learning for these kids. In Washington, middle-schoolers were paid for a portfolio of five different metrics, including attendance and good behavior. If they hit perfect marks in every category, they could make $100 every two weeks. In Washington, each school got to choose three of the payment metrics, and some of the elements ended up being outcomes like test scores. But the students were also paid on the basis of attendance and behavior—*two actions that are under their direct control.*

And in Dallas, paying second-graders to read books significantly boosted their reading-comprehension scores on standardized tests at the end of the year —and those kids seemed to continue to do better the next year, even after the rewards stopped. Schools in Dallas had the simplest scheme and the one targeting the youngest children: every time second-graders read a book and successfully completed a computerized quiz about it, they earned $2. In Dallas, paying kids to read books—something almost all of them can do—made a big difference. It may have also helped that the kids in Dallas were the youngest in the experiment, making them more receptive to change in habits (Ripley, *Time*, April, 8, 2010).

It is not hard to reach the next conclusion: At best, the results were mixed; at worst, they can diminish learning over the long term. When older students are extrinsically rewarded with incentives for reading, as in a commonly used, for-profit program entitled the 100-Book Challenge, marketed by The American Reading Company, most beyond the second grade will not pick up a 101st, let alone learn to love reading. All they learned to love was getting an extrinsic reward. The American Reading Company certainly got its extrinsic reward, regardless of the success rate of its program.

What too many education reformers must learn (non-algorithmically) is that they are going in the opposite direction to where science is pointing when it comes to learning and engagement in the classroom, because they neglect the three keys to genuine motivation: autonomy, mastery, and purpose.

SELF-DETERMINATION THEORY

This argues we have to meet three innate psychological needs in order to be happily motivated and productive. These needs are: competence, autonomy, and relatedness. Edward Deci and Richard Ryan point out that for these to function, we must have environments that foster them. They and other Self Determination Theory (SDT) scholars have written hundreds of papers that have shown that when our inner drives to be autonomous, self-determined, and connected are liberated (Pink 2009), human achievement is at its greatest level.

For years, most institutions operated under the Frederick Winslow Taylor assumption of a century ago. This assumption presumed that the masses were drones that badly needed coercion, strict instruction, precise direction, and threats with punishment because they fundamentally disliked work and would avoid it if they could. "Work," Taylor stated, "consists of simple, not particularly interesting tasks. The only way to get people to do them is to incentivize them properly and monitor them carefully". That is what we often call classroom management. (http://www.

evancarmichael.com/Leadership/2038/Motivating-People-at-Work--The-Power-of-Intrinsic-Motivation.html).

Douglas McGregor, in his 1960 book, *The Human Side of Enterprise,* argued for the opposite. McGregor's theories state that for people, work is "as natural as play or rest." Under the proper conditions, they will accept and actually seek out responsibility. Think of young children before we have ruined them.

In education today, it seems as if our reformers are reforming us back to Taylor. Their belief, as McGregor pointed out fifty years ago, in the "mediocrity of the masses" (as supported by empirical testing) has fostered a systemic, algorithmic approach that has made "mediocrity the ceiling of what can be achieved." It has become more "no child too far ahead" than "No Child Left Behind."

This nineteenth-century operating system is based on the assumption that behavior is ignited more by extrinsic reward than intrinsic motivation. The problem is, as Pink points out, "If we want to strengthen our [schools], get beyond our decade[s] of underachievement, and address the inchoate sense that something has gone wrong in our businesses, [our schools], our lives, and our world, we need to move from...that Tayloresque operating system to one that more readily accepts and believes in the power of intrinsic motivation" (Pink 2009).

Extrinsic motivation works best when the assignment neither inspires passion nor requires deep thinking, problem solving, or a more creative approach. It works best when the goal of the assignment is not to instill a long-range love of a subject or practice. In short, it can be used to learn to do simple, routine things. Extrinsic rewards work best when accompanied by the answers to these three, basic, human questions:

- "Why do we have to do this?"

   Give the rationale for why it is necessary.

- "Why is this so boring?"

   Admit it is. Show empathy and connect the extrinsic reward.

- "Do we have to do it that way?"

   - No. Let them use autonomy to achieve the required goal.

If, however, the assignment requires heuristic thinking, is creative and problem solving, or is intended to instill an interest in or love for something--think very carefully. A classroom environment must already be one where baseline rewards are seen as sufficient and fair. The classroom must be a congenial place to work, and all students must feel they can be autonomous, have an opportunity to gain mastery, and have a purpose in doing this assignment. Then, a teacher's task is to provide a sense of significance and need (urgency) and get out of the way, except to facilitate.

How about rewards now?

- Surprise them with a post-assignment reward.
    - It should be unexpected and offered only after successful completion of the task.

- Consider nontangible rewards.
    - As Deci (1999) pointed out, "positive feedback can have an enhancing effect on intrinsic motivation."
    - However, that positive feedback or praise must provide specific information about effort and strategy, not goal achievement.

As researchers delved into the categories of extrinsically versus intrinsically motivated behaviors, they found the real key to success was the degree of control versus the degree of autonomy. Deci and Ryan (2008) found that controlled motivation involves pressure and demand from external sources to achieve specific outcomes, whereas autonomous motivation involves having a full sense of choice and will.

So what? (An intrinsically motivating question.) Autonomous motivation has been found by many recent studies to "promote greater conceptual understanding, better grades, enhanced persistence in school and in sporting activities" (Deci and Ryan, 2008). Paul Baard, of Fordham University (2004), found that this carries over into the workplace as well.

PINK'S "THE FOUR TS" (FROM THE ESSENTIALS OF AUTONOMY):

TASK (WHAT THEY DO)

The freedom to choose one's own task creates a huge amount of intrinsic motivation. Many top businesses (for example, Google) give their employees 20 percent of their time to devote to their own projects. G-mail is an example. It was invented during one Googleite's 20 percent of free time. Top progressive schools, regardless of socioeconomic backgrounds, allow students the ability to work on autonomous projects. Sudbury Valley, Puget Sound Community, and Montessori schools are examples. The WISE program for Individualized Senior Experiences (www.wiservices. org) is an example of how high schools can opt for this type of learning for their seniors.

TIME (WHEN THEY DO IT)

Herein lies a dichotomy. Without sovereignty over our time, it is extremely hard to have autonomy, and how can we do that in classrooms that are ruled by bells, periods, units, tests, etc. Think about creating "The Process Is the Product" projects, where designing the process is as much an integral part of the project as the content or product. Of course, these projects include a series of deadlines, but students manage the time, not the teachers. Let students figure out how to develop a valuable skill (*time management*). This has to be learned by doing.

TECHNIQUE (HOW THEY DO IT)

Teachers have to fight the urge to be in control--to know exactly how to do it right, and pass that knowledge. How many times have we been told to, "Show (model) and tell them what to do and how to do it, then let them do it"? What has that achieved? Have they felt the satisfaction of achieving a creative solution to a vexing problem? Have they practiced and internalized this important process, or have they done robotic "copy-and-paste" learning, which we abhor.

TEAM (WITH WHOM THEY DO IT)

Simply stated, people in self-organized teams work better and are more satisfied. However, students uninitiated to this process of group work depend on teachers to help them figure out the possible roles until they can do it for themselves. Unfortunately, teachers too often rely on the standard models for "teamwork." Instead we give them a boring, less successful, robotic method, "Wack-A-Mole" approach. They think they have to do it the way they have always done it, especially when it comes to the presentation. Teachers must have students search for novel ways of dividing their labor to allow for their strengths more equitably, not equally, so the results are more inspired, creative, and enjoyable. Stressing this type of autonomy does not mean doing away with the other omnipotent "A" word, "accountability." Kids want to be held accountable for their work. It simply means using more authentic assessments to measure it.

AUTONOMY BEGETS ENGAGEMENT BEGETS MASTERY.

Autonomy leads to increased engagement. Engagement leads to creativity and problem solving, and thus to better learning. There is less need for what is commonly called classroom management that subtracts from autonomy and leads to compliance rather than creative problem solving. One doesn't need to manage engaged students. Engaged students are better learners. Better learners are more able to gain mastery. "Only engagement can lead to mastery" (Pink 2009).

Mastery is the desire to get better and better at something that matters. Mihaly Csikszentmihali of the University of Chicago and the Claremont Graduate University found, as early as the 1970s, that creativity is linked with play. In this type of experience, the activity (yes, the quality of the activity does matter) is its own reward. Csikszentmihali called this feeling "flow." Athletes might talk about being in flow (being in a zone) when goals are clear and feedback immediate. Everything clicks. Success is astronomical.

A major source of frustration, felt by teachers and students alike, is the frequent conflict between what we can do and what we are told we must do. When what we can do exceeds what we must do, the result is boredom. When what we must do exceeds what we can do, the result is anxiety. Look around US classrooms. How many kids are bored? Anxious? How many are "in a zone"? There lies the challenge for us. How do we create environments and assignments where flow can be the norm? Why must we? Because flow is the prerequisite for mastery, and mastery is what we want our students to achieve.

MASTERY IS IN THE MIND.

As Tug McGraw of the Amazing Mets of 1973 said, "Ya gotta believe." What we believe about ourselves shapes what we can achieve. Carol Dweck of Stanford University posits that if we believe we can't get smarter, we won't, and that if we believe we can, we will. Schools and classrooms set the stage for these beliefs by using one of two systems regarding goals: performance goals and learning goals. Unfortunately, this is another way NCLB/RTTT have led to what I call "proficiently advanced mediocrity." It calls for performance goals that limit one's intellectual growth, and therefore limit achievement of mastery, while achieving mediocrity.

Dweck found that children paid in performance goals (extrinsic motivators) effectively solved straightforward problems, but had difficulty when they had to apply techniques to real-world applications or similar problems worded slightly differently. In contrast, she also found that students "paid" in intrinsic learning goals were able to apply their knowledge to new sets of similar, yet not identical problems. The first group of students was advanced in their mediocrity. The second was well on their way to expanding abilities and consistently seek far more inventive strategies to problem solving.

Mastery is hard. Mastery includes "grit"--a perseverance, persistence, and passion to achieve long-term, not short-term goals like passing standardized tests. There is a strong relationship between caring, passion, effort, and mastery. If you care about something intrinsically, you will put forward the effort to achieve it. To paraphrase basketball great Dr. J (Julius Irving), [being really good at something] "is doing the things you love to do, on the days you don't feel like doing them."

Mastery is a quest. We must prepare our students for that quest. Preparing them robotically using extrinsic rewards to succeed on standardized tests just doesn't make kids believe that star is reachable, or that it is even in their universe.

Mastery evokes curiosity. How do we get back to childlike curiosity? It is our job to reteach our students to do what once came naturally. We must create classrooms and assignments that allow them to use their innate abilities to investigate their environment in the endless pursuit of mastery, not the mediocre level of proficient competence sought after by the "reform" advocated by test reformers.

THE SIGNIFICANCE OF PURPOSE.

To achieve this intrinsic motivation, we not only need autonomy and mastery, we need purpose. Teachers must be able to answer that question kids often ask, "What are we doin' this for?" If the answers are simply for a good grade or to prepare for the standardized exam, we are exacerbating the problem, not solving it. Kids need to know there is a real purpose to the assignment or work. Purpose energizes. Kids are more motivated pursuing purpose.

Obviously, not all assignments can be purpose-centered assignments. But, if planned right, some assignments can become prerequisites for purpose-centered assignments. More rudimentary, skill-building assignments have a purpose. If we address them as building blocks necessary to be better able to work at the really big purpose-centered assignment, "capstone," or culminating assignment students will succeed. Allowing students to work on something that is meaningful to them is *key*.

This can be done in many ways. School districts can make these processes the norm just as easily as a major corporation (Google). The benefits more than offset the "lost" time. A school can have a program where students get academic credit for working on a project of their own choosing (WISE). Classroom teachers can devise projects where students can apply the skills they have learned to a particular purpose that is important to them, in or out of the classroom. It's easy. We just "gotta believe."

CONSCIOUS SKILLS

Process is the key to everything. Understanding why and how we do what we do makes us better. As a football coach, one of the greatest lessons I learned from other coaches was that players played better when they not only knew their roles, but also how they fit into the greater scheme. Players routinely did better at performing a particular technique (a series of repetitive, muscle-memory-led actions, depending on the position and play) when they knew what their buddies on each side of them were doing and why.

Similarly, I have seen countless times over the years that students do better when they understand why and how to use particular skills in certain situations. Groups perform better when they understand the why and how of the group process they are using for that particular activity. Often, they perform best when they are given the autonomy to devise their own process (as long as it meets the standards devised for the activity).

Another football lesson is the acronym the most successful coaches tell themselves when they overthink things: K.I.S.S. (Keep It Simple, Stupid). It is a basic reminder to us all to slow down and to work smarter, not harder. The most effective and efficient way from point *A* to point *B* is a straight line. Similarly, the most successful coaches in sports are often the ones who were not superstars. In fact, many were journeymen, bench sitters, or backups. They studied the game. It didn't come easily to them.

This introduces the concept of unconscious versus conscious thinking. Highly skilled and naturally talented people tend to unconsciously "just do it." They don't understand the process. They can't break their talent down into the smallest techniques and skills the rest of us have to struggle to do. If they can't, while they may be highly skilled, they make terrible coaches, or teachers.

The best teachers, like the best coaches, regardless of the innate talents they may possess, learn how to break down the processes of teaching and learning into conscious skills that they can pass on to others clearly, simply, and transparently. A brief sports example: A young man keeps dropping a football thrown to him. The unconsciously guided or uninformed coach will say something like, "watch the ball into your hands." That sounds like good advice. But what does that actually mean? The kid thinks, "I've **been** doing that." The kid is failing, and so is the coach.

The good coach will describe and model the actual steps "watch the ball into your hands" is composed of. See the release of the ball from the quarterback. When you first see the ball, find *one small spot* on the ball on which to *focus* and *follow it* into your hands. Then, tuck the ball under your arm, seeing the ball all the way into the tuck. In fact, they are taught a new word, *catchntuck,* because the whole process must include all parts to be successful. Often, it seems interscholastic teams have higher standards for proficiency than academic classes. We should take notice.

So what happened here? The coach clearly broke down the skill of catching into its basic steps. Each step was clearly labeled, and a memorable or catchy name was introduced. The best teachers do this. The naturally talented ones do it unconsciously. Most learn how to do it--consciously. The best teacher trainers train teachers to teach conscious skills.

Lemov (2010) knows this is a key ingredient to successful teaching. He refers to four general steps to teach process: First, naming the steps (as did our receivers coach) makes complex skills transparent. Second, keep the steps as few as possible, and as clear as possible (K.I.S.S.). Third, the proper sequencing of steps is important in education. Once taught how to recreate those steps they can figure out any similar problem. Fourth, it has to be memorable. This is why kids must learn to make, not take, clear and organized notes. Look at the action verbs. *To make* means to create. *To take* means to steal. Which do you want them to learn to do? The action of writing notes on paper actually reinforces memory. Looking at prescribed, worksheet handouts does not. Even the most attractive handouts only get looked at and then put away and forgotten (or lost).

Other ways to make things memorable include creating your own catchy words or phrases that act as memory triggers. *Catchntuck* is an example. Rhymes are examples. Song lyrics work. Word substitutions work as well. Think about how the Rolling Stones lyric, "You can't always get what you want," describes the concepts of scarcity and opportunity cost in economics. Posters and signs can be functional decoration unless there is too much as is often too the case. Too much causes visual overload. There is so much to see nothing is noticed. Remember to K.I.S.S. your classroom walls as well.

A corollary to K.I.S.S. is "Less is More." This is at the very core of the debate in education between the NCLB/RTTT corporate education "deformers" and classroom teachers. Teachers know the importance of understanding. They know *depth* is key to *breadth*. They also understand the importance of time and slowing it down when necessary to make sure kids "get it." They understand the virtues of repetition. The best coaches consistently talk of the value of "reps" in learning skills. The best teachers know the significance of teaching process as well as content. That takes time. You cannot rush a class to master process, and, therefore, content. If you rush, the chances are only the students who take to it more unconsciously will be successful.

Whatever happened to real science and the scientific method? When did worksheets become more important learning tools than labs? I wasn't a big science guy--although I went to the Bronx High School of Science--but the thing I remember most was how potassium and water don't mix. In fact, it is a violent reaction. Why? I jumped higher than my usual "white guys can't jump" when, during a Chemistry lab, I dropped a potassium pellet into a beaker of water. That was over forty years ago. Who thinks today's rote, prepare for the test worksheet would make me remember that? Labs and experiential learning take time. That is what science education should be.

Finally, depth takes time. In the sciences and the humanities (ELA and social studies), reading for understanding of why and how is more important than who, what, when, and where. Who, what, when, and where are more easily learned (and remembered long-term) if students realize they are tools to discuss how and why. Learning to read carefully, a skill in itself, means learning to read slowly enough to understand. Skim reading should not be the norm, if we want kids to retain and understand material of any type.

Analysis is a skill most kids are not asked to be proficient in (especially in poorer schools). Yet, it is the most important part of learning and understanding. It takes time to analyze, simply because "to analyze" means to "break down." How can you break down and rush at the same time? Good analysis leads students to good synthesis. Putting something together in your own words...takes time. It takes understanding. It takes depth. Students must be taught the conscious skills included in analysis and synthesis. Aren't those parts of the scientific method as well? These take time to be learned and practiced.

SKILLED PRACTITIONERS

Student-centered classrooms are teacher conducted. Imagine an orchestra whose conductor just stood there. Imagine a team whose coach stood silently on the sidelines, offering no support, encouragement, or guidance. Now, imagine a classroom with the teacher just standing there after handing out the "work." Oh, you say, you don't have to imagine it. You suffered through it? Too often, in the valiant and positive attempt of ridding classrooms of the boring-lecture-and-control-freak teachers, we have thrown out the baby with the bath water. In fact, there is always time for stimulating discussion and good note making. In fact, the best student-centered classrooms are very covertly teacher controlled. Let us call these classrooms teacher "conducted" or "coached."

The key ingredient once again is planning, regardless of the type of lesson or portion of a lesson. Technology-based, inquiry-based, discussion-based, lecture-based, group-work-based lessons are all orchestrated, choreographed, blocked, or game-planned, (depending on the particular metaphor of choice) with the teacher as an integral player-coach. Teachers are fearless leaders in the trenches with their troops to succeed in the quest for academic victory. "I love the smell of silly putty in the morning; it smells like victory," if you are a first-grade teacher, perhaps (with apologies to Francis Ford Coppola and Robert Duvall).

Planning involves more than just a good lesson plan's content, questions, and activities. It involves the teacher knowing where she will be and what she will do at all times. For example, seating plans should allow easy teacher circulation around the room to monitor, cajole, encourage, supervise, admonish, and, of course, conduct the public speaking orchestration a class is engaged in. Teachers should own the room and conduct the business that takes place in it. It should be a natural extension of their personality. Their presence any place at any time must be the norm. Movement is proactive, not reactive. Those movements are key to a covertly controlled classroom.

Great teachers dance. They float. They jump and even climb on desks. They are not afraid to be "crazier" than their students are. They entertain. They keep 'em engaged. It's all part of the aura. Leader or victim? Motivator or manager? Engaging movement gives power. Having eyes on everything prevents what Lemov (2010) euphemistically calls "opportunistic behavior." Having the sneakiest of kids know they are being watched provides a tremendous, strategic advantage.

Speaking of strategy...

SUN TZU'S ART OF WAR

> "The general who wins a battle makes many calculations in his temple ere the battle is fought. The general who loses a battle makes but few calculations beforehand."

- "Those who are skilled in producing surprises will win. Such tacticians are as versatile as the changes in heaven and earth. They are like the five music notes; combinations that produce endless melodies, like the five colours: mixture that produces a variety of beautiful objects."

- "He will win whose army is animated by the same spirit throughout all its ranks."

- "When the common soldiers are too strong and their officers too weak, the result is *insubordination*. When the officers are too strong and the common soldiers too weak, the result is collapse."

That is the real "strategic plan." Just as movement is "planned," so are "what ifs." You must know ahead of time what you will do when plan "*A*" falters, or a student doesn't do what you thought he or she would. Do you have the wherewithal to react positively in that moment without breaking a sweat? Those moments define you as a teacher and leader.

In June 2010, a student drowned at a Long Island, New York beach because inexperienced teachers didn't consider a plan *B*. Their school trip ended up at a beach without lifeguards. Why didn't they look at the new problem and get back on the bus and go to a beach with lifeguards ten minutes away? More importantly, why didn't they ask that question ahead of time? A child died. A family and community mourned. They lost their jobs. Why? They didn't analyze the situation carefully and ask the right questions. They were unprepared for the unexpected. If you expect the unexpected, you can handle what arises with confidence. Prepare for it.

AN ENGAGING EXCHANGE

The best teachers are communicators. They are listeners. They can figure out in a heartbeat how to help a student who is dumbfounded, misconstruing, or misspeaking. How they accomplish that depends on the particular student. They need to know their kids and be prepared and able to use a variety of means, starting with the simple idea of careful listening. Suppose a kid speaks up in class and makes an error. Too often, teachers will, for the sake of speed, make the correction and move on. What has that done? The kid still feels dumb; the class is less likely to remember it, because they always remember less when the adult says it.

The best teachers know how to respond when a kid makes an error. At some point, good teachers consciously or unconsciously learn to conceptualize what they teach, and as quick as a wink, figure out how to lead this mistaken student to the promised land of "I figured it out." A quick series of clues, hints, and probing questions follow that allow him to succeed. Consciously, we figure out how much he needs. How far away is he from the right answer? Was it just a misspoken answer? Will repeating his answer give him the "oops" moment to self-correct? Can a simple example do it? A context clue? A rule of thumb? Maybe, an obviously wrong possibility is a clue. If nothing else works...ask another kid to help. Ahh, he's gotten it. We can quickly move on. That whole exchange may have taken thirty seconds.

Benjamin Franklin said, "Tell me, and I forget. Teach me, and I remember. Involve me, and I learn." Students learn best by action and discussion. How much talking should a teacher do? As little as possible. Your role is a moderator, a conductor, and a facilitator. How much should the kids do? They should do as much as possible: talking and interacting with teachers less than with each other, as a full class or in groups. Students are participants. The verb is *to participate*. It is why participation should be a major part of grades, at least 20 percent. Don't we meet and participate in class far more than we test or write? Therefore, isn't it the best place to assess student understanding and knowledge? Students get that. They see participation as a behavior to be expected and rewarded.

Therein lies the rub. In the top schools in the nation (usually the wealthiest and whitest), this usually isn't much of a controversy, unless imposed on them by bureaucrats. (See "The Test Mess," James Traub, *The New York Times*, April 7, 2002.) Students who have the elite universities as their goals are taught even in elementary school the steps of analysis and synthesis. They are taught depth more so than breadth (depending on the subject). Time for in-depth activities is built into the curricula for students of all abilities.

One way ninth-grade English students in Scarsdale High School are taught Shakespeare is via a Shakespeare festival. Each class performs one scene from the play they are all learning for each other in a daylong assembly program. That takes weeks of preparation, but those actors learn Shakespeare (and perhaps an appreciation of the bard) from the inside out.

Now, compare that to the minimally proficient standards to which we are holding urban students (Black, Hispanic, the poorest immigrants) "accountable." Their proficiency standards do not prepare them for any elite university. These standards barely prepare them for functional literacy during a time when our nation's economic restructuring has all but made basic working-class jobs unavailable. Those that are available barely pay a decent wage.

CHAPTER 2:

WHAT'S GOING ON HERE?

WHO WILL TEACH?

"A new survey paints a troubling portrait of the American educator: Teacher job satisfaction has hit its lowest point in a quarter of a century, and 75 percent of principals believe their jobs have become too complex.

The findings are part of the MetLife *Survey of the American Teacher: Challenges for School Leadership.* Conducted annually since 1984, the survey polled representative sampling of 1,000 teachers and 500 principals in K-12 schools across the country.

"Only 39 percent of teachers described themselves as very satisfied with their jobs on the latest survey. That's a 23-percentage point plummet since 2008, and a drop of five percentage points just over the past year. Factors contributing to lower job satisfaction included working in schools where the budgets, opportunities for professional development, and time for collaboration with colleagues have all been sent to the chopping block. Stress levels are also up, with half of all teachers describing themselves as under great stress several days per week, compared with a third of teachers in 1985."

Given those numbers, who wants to teach besides TFA corps members who know all they have to do is last two years then go on their way to their real vocations? Teaching must be more of a profession for our most creative and ambitious 20-somethings. We must market the opportunities to become an autonomous, creative professional with room for growth. In addition, there needs to be obvious material incentives. To its credit, TFA has started to get more of our best and brightest to become teachers. But, how do we get them to stay?

Finance and law draw many potential great teachers away from the profession. The highest, state average, starting salary for a teacher is approximately $40,000. The highest, state average salary for a teacher of any experience is approximately $65,000, the average, starting salary for a first-year lawyer. A first-year analyst in investment banking averages double that, and a third-year associate with an MBA averages $350,000 in compensation (careers-in-finance.com). At the same time, the top 10 percent of teachers in the country have an average salary range from $75,190 to $80,970. Even in Scarsdale, one of the highest-paid teaching staffs in the nation, the average salary was $95,840 back in 2006-07 (*Source:* 2006-2007 Contract Analysis conducted by the Negotiations Clearinghouse, Putnam, Westchester and Rockland Counties). It is now over $100,000, but that still doesn't come close to the figures attracting the best and brightest to the private sector. Apparently, our best and brightest prefer the big bucks to job prestige in national rankings. Why? Among the elite, the prestige is in making the big bucks. Good teachers often tell their students and their own children not to join the profession. Why are teachers paid so little in comparison?

Without big bucks, and no military draft to avoid (yes, that did bring a large number of very talented baby boomers to teaching in the late '60s), the number of good, talented teaching candidates will continue to decline. But unlike then when the vast majority stayed teachers, today's college students are apt to go the quick temporary route via TFA. They cannot get good jobs anymore and use their brief experience to pad their resumes before they leave to go on their eventual career path. After their two-year stint, only about 20 percent of TFA Corps Members were still teaching in public schools in 2010.

The major problem is strictly the supply and demand of good replacement teachers. What are the chances of replacing retiring or a bad experienced teacher with a better, inexperienced one? A new study, according to Emily Johnson in her August 10, 2010 article in *The Dartmouth*, found that in their first two years, TFA-trained teachers do "significantly less well" in raising reading and math test scores than beginning teachers with traditional teaching certifications. Certainly, programs like Teach

For America are helping recruit new, bright candidates for jobs in our worst schools. Yet, they come with caveats. First, although very bright, are Teach For Americans talented and tough enough to handle the kind of nonacademic rigor they will face? Some. Second, are they being properly trained? Only a few. Third, will they last? No. Only 20 percent last more than two years. Then, new ones have to be hired all over again. Is that what we are looking for?

It is also true that bad teachers are in the system. However, the reasons for this are far more complex than the media and policy makers who have the media in their hands make it out to be. Teachers in the public schools are protected by union-obtained job security for good reason. Tenure was secured because in the old pre-union days, good teachers who fought against bad administrators were fired. Unfortunately, tenure is claimed to be the major reason bad teachers aren't fired. Most good teachers will tell you it should be easier to get rid of those who stain the profession. Unions and districts can and do work together to work out these issues. State legislatures can update outmoded procedures and hire more hearing officers to speed the process along without losing due process.

The underlying problem is the politicization of the process. It has been too adversarial. Teachers who offer working solutions have been ignored because they have been lumped into being part of "The Union," and therefore positioned by politicians and the media as the enemy opposed to education reform. What the policy makers refuse to see is that many teachers don't care about choosing sides. They aren't the ardent unionists that politicians and reporters make them out to be. They believe in the right to organize and have unions or associations fight for fair and efficient due process, good salaries, and the same medical coverage and pensions as congressmen. They are on the side of the kids and have successfully worked with them for years. In short, policy makers need to listen to teachers, and stop fighting with "The Union."

A *union*, by definition, is a collective bargaining organization that protects its workers from abuses and attempts to gain the best salary and benefits for its members. It is also true, too, that unions, because of their collective nature, stifle individual members. However, that depends on the relationship between management and labor. I have worked in three school districts. Two did not respect the professionalism of their teachers, and one did. It was no surprise that in the latter district, the highest degree of innovative and inspirational teaching took place. It also was the district where the union and board worked most closely together to benefit kids. When districts value teachers, hire carefully, pay well, give good benefits, and treat them as valued members of their community, the district's children reap the benefits.

Who do we want as teachers? What kind of energy will they bring to the classroom? How well will they motivate students to want to learn and learn how to learn? If those happen, then whatever the techniques, that teacher has become a great teacher. Not every college graduate is cut out to teach. Not every second-career teacher is cut out to teach, regardless of his or her innate intelligence, GPA, or previous career success. Only those with specific talents can become gifted teachers who, working with a variety of learned tools and techniques, will produce students, not simply on the path to college, but rather on the path to postgraduate worlds of work and study.

As Emeritus Columbia University Professor Frank Smith has observed, "the best kind of education" is about distinctive and impassioned teaching, the kind that will engage and excite students. Often, it is the least orthodox that are the greatest teachers. As one of my great teachers told a class of mine in high school, "Think about what *outstanding* really means... standing out from and being above the crowd." What is an exceptional teacher? *Exceptional* has come to mean best or brightest, but doesn't it really mean to be the exception? The one who stands out from the crowd? Those are the great teachers--the ones we remember. Teachers teach. Well-trained teachers teach better. Great teachers change lives.

Weren't your best teachers those who had practical wisdom? Weren't they the ones who had character, along with certain principles and virtues that you may have not appreciated at the time? Weren't they the ones who obviously loved their work and you as a result? And weren't they the ones who almost always seemed to do the right things for the right reasons, the right way? Scripts and rules and models strictly followed cannot replace what the best teachers have most...practical wisdom. There is no substitute for it.

It's no secret why districts like Scarsdale attract and usually get the best teachers, while urban districts like New York City schools don't.

It wasn't always that way. In fact, when I started in 1970, the opposite may have been true. Many excellent teachers left New York City because they saw the writing on the wall. The pay scales became far better in the suburbs. Parental involvement is far more positive. Socioeconomic factors that improve student scores are clearly evident. The level of professional treatment, although varied by district, was better than in New York City. Yet, the same old bugaboo persists.

I recently had a conversation with someone who strongly believed and argued, "Lower student scores are produced by students with poor teachers, and higher student scores are produced by students with good teachers." I simply asked her one question. "Did I become a better teacher when I changed jobs from a Bronx high school with poorer test results to Scarsdale High School?" She was clearly stumped, but refused to change her mind.

HOW NOT TO FIX THINGS

A story in the New York Times (February, 28, 2013) sums up what is currently a norm. It happened at what was once Taft High School where I student taught almost 45 years ago. Years ago it was broken up into bite sized schools as per the policy of Mayor Michael Bloomberg following the Bill and Melinda Gates agenda to break up big "poorly functioning" high schools. According to Al Baker's story, "Closing schools and replacing them has been the hallmark of education reform efforts all around the country, promoted by the Obama administration and embraced by mayor Michael R. Bloomberg, who has shuttered 142 of them since taking office in 2002 and, in his final year is moving to close 24 more."

One of the new schools created 10 years ago was named after a young teacher, Jonathan M Levin, who was killed by one of his former students five years earlier. Over the subsequent years initial hopes were dashed. Renovations and a new athletic field fell into disrepair. New technology became outmoded and unused. Finally the school sank to NYC's 5th lowest in graduation rate, 31 percent. So the NYC DOE decided to close it and open another replacement school.

What happened over the past 10 years? The story of Taft is a micro-cosm of this policy. Six small schools replaced one big one. Four of the six small schools have failed. One is being "phased out" (the euphemism for closing). One received 2 "D"s on NYC School Progress reports, another received 2 "C's. These two should be closed according to NYC criteria. The Levin School is about to be phased out. What about the other 2? One, it seems only admits students performing at or above grade level and the other was found to manipulate the numbers of students it had enrolled to make it look like it was more successful than it actually was.

Stories like this happen all across NYC and other similar "failing" big city school districts. In addition, many of the newer schools (most often charter) that appear to be more successful do so by limiting admission to large numbers of the high needs students, leaving them to the older, failing schools. How many of these stories does the public know about unless they are active parents involved in their school? How much is heard of the glossed over "inconvenient truths"? Not much.

I am so fed up I am even willing to quote Spiro Agnew, "The nattering nabobs of negativism" who influence education policy need to be halted. These policies must end. Good schools attract good and great teachers. Great teachers change lives. Tests don't. Why, then, are we so linked to tests (and poorly devised ones, at that) as the sole measure of teacher and school accountability? Several authors have theories. Many (like Diane Ravitch) point out that over the past two decades education policy has fallen into the hands of policy makers bred and influenced by major cor-porations and the foundations they support. The Gates Foundation and The Fordham (not University) Institute are two good examples.

They still live by the standard of industrial America developed a full century ago by Frederick W. Taylor. Captains of industry (robber barons) supported scientific management, as it was called, in order to make their employees more productive. Today's policy makers want to turn teach-ers into industrial employees, churning students out like Ford workers churned out Model T's. Taylor and his followers turned efficiency into the justification for such changes. The industrial leaders of the day believed implementation of scientific management would benefit both workers and society at-large. Today's policy makers have bought it hook, line, and sinker. Look at a recent example. For ten years New York City schools have been totally controlled by a Mayor and financial captain of industry (Michael Bloomberg) and his henchmen: Joel Klein, Kathie Black (what a disastrous three months), and now Dennis Walcott. Nowhere more than in New York City is "Taylorism" being used to run schools. Furthermore, there is an international organization to foster this approach to parallel the global corporate economic movement. It is called G.E.R.M. (Global Education Reform Movement). Pasi Sahlberg, author of *Finnish Lessons: What Can the World Learn from Educational Change in Finland*, tells us:

> G.E.R.M. has emerged since the 1980s and has increasingly become adopted as educational reform orthodoxy within many education systems throughout the world, including in the US, England, Australia and some transition countries. Tellingly, G.E.R.M. is often promoted through the interests of international development agencies and private enterprises through their interventions in national education reforms and policy formulation.
>
> Since the 1980s, at least five globally common features of education policies and reform principles have been employed to try to improve the quality of education and fix the apparent problems in public education systems.
>
> First is *standardization* of education. Outcomes-based education reform became popular in the 1980s, followed by standards-based education policies in the 1990s. A widely accepted–and generally unquestioned–belief among policy makers and education reformers is that setting clear and sufficiently high performance standards for schools, teachers, and students will necessarily improve the quality of expected outcomes. Enforcement of external testing and evaluation systems to assess how well these standards have been attained emerged originally from standards-oriented education policies. Since the late 1980s, centrally prescribed curricula, with detailed and often ambitious performance targets, frequent testing of students and teachers, and test-based

accountability have characterized a homogenization of education policies worldwide, promising standardized solutions at increasingly lower cost for those desiring to improve school quality and effectiveness.

A second common feature of G.E.R.M. is *focus on core subjects* in school, in other words, on literacy and numeracy. Basic student knowledge and skills in reading, writing, and mathematics are elevated as prime targets and indices of education reforms. As a consequence of accepting international student assessment surveys, such as PISA, TIMSS, and PIRLS as criteria of good educational performance, reading, mathematical, and scientific literacy have now become the main determinants of perceived success or failure of pupils, teachers, schools, and entire education systems. This is happening [at] the expense of social studies, arts, music, and physical education that are diminishing in many school curricula.

The third characteristic that is easily identifiable in global education reforms is *the search for low-risk ways to reach learning goals*. This minimizes experimentation, reduces use of alternative pedagogical approaches, and limits risk taking in schools and classrooms. The higher the test-result stakes, the lower the degree of freedom in experimentation and risk taking in classroom learning.

The fourth globally observable trend in educational reform is *use of corporate management models* as a main driver of improvement. This process where educational policies and ideas are lent and borrowed from the business world is often motivated by national hegemony and economic profit, rather than by moral goals of human development. Faith in educational change through innovations bought and sold from outside the system undermines and paralyzes teachers' and schools' attempts to learn from the past and also to learn from each other.

The fifth global trend is adoption of *test-based account-ability policies* for schools. In doing so, school perfor-mance—especially raising student achievement—is closely tied to processes of accrediting, promoting, inspecting, and, ultimately, rewarding or punishing schools and teachers. Success or failure of schools and teachers is often determined by standardized tests and external teacher evaluations that devote attention to limited aspects of schooling, such as student achievement in mathematical and reading literacy, exit examination results, or intended teacher classroom behavior.

None of these elements of G.E.R.M. have been adopted in Finland in the ways that they have within education policies of many other nations, for instance, in the United States and England. (Sahlberg 2011)

Finland places at the top of all international studies. Where are we? I see two notable problems with this approach. First, kids aren't identi-cal, mass-produced Model-Ts. They are human beings. Second, teachers aren't industrial machines. They are professionals, like doctors, lawyers, accountants, and yes, even MBA businessmen. They need to be treated as such.

In the early 20th century, according to Jonathan Rees of the University of Southern Colorado, teachers were also required to document their teach-ing activities in order to minimize "waste." Poor, public school students were being managed and trained to become obedient factory workers, not thinking managers or innovators. Thinking creatively and problem solving were learned by the upper classes in private schools. It seems not much has changed in a century. However, since many of Taylor's dis-ciples in education were not educators themselves, they seldom tried to tell teachers what or how to teach. Scientific management in the modern classroom, as it rears its ugly head today, does not respect the idea that teachers know what to teach their students or how best to teach it. Passing the test is thought of in the same way as housebreaking the dog, or train-ing the factory worker. Did anyone notice we don't do factories anymore?

Let's look further. Rees notes, "Forcing teachers to address content that can be measured in standardized tests and to avoid more analytical material hinders learning. Doing so also devalues the profession of teaching in the same way that scientific management devalued the role of skilled craft workers in American factories." He found early evidence of this in Richard Callahan's 1962 book, *Education and the Cult of Efficiency*. Callahan states that students were viewed as workers. "The ability to add at a speed of 65 combinations per minute, with an accuracy of 94 percent," wrote one reformer, "is as definite a specification as can be set up for any aspect of the work of the steel plant" (John Franklin Bobbitt quoted in Callahan, 1962:81).

To quote Rees,

> The best example of Frederick Taylor's ideas at work in education today are high-stakes standardized tests--tests which have a significant effect on funding for schools and the careers of individual students. Although these exams can create enormous tension for students and administrators, it is teachers whose lives are most affected by them. Thanks to mounting pressure to get students to score high marks, teachers must concentrate on teaching the curriculum chosen by test-designers, rather than local school boards or themselves.

> Furthermore, because preparation for multiple-choice or short-answer questions that make up these tests require[s] only a superficial understanding of complex material in order to answer them correctly, they provide no rationale for teachers to reinforce more complex concepts that take additional effort for students to understand. Since teachers do not need to teach or themselves understand abstract concepts that cannot be measured on standardized tests, creative pedagogy is not rewarded in this new regime, and the quality of learning among students inevitably suffers.

Like skilled workers in industrializing America, teachers'
prerogatives are disappearing, and the talents that they
once utilized daily are increasingly no longer called upon.
(Rees 2001)

Let's examine another catachrestic truth. "If you test a child on basic
math and reading skills, and you're teaching to the test, you're teaching
math and reading. And that's the whole idea" (Bush, G.W. 2001). It was
President Bush who, with the support of both conservative Republicans
and liberal Democrats like Senator Ted Kennedy, passed the No Child Left
Behind Act. That Act is the basis of what President Obama's Secretary of
Education, Arne Duncan's created called Race to the Top. This version of
educational reform is really NCLB II.

Both No Child Left Behind and Race to the Top have made standardized testing the single most important assessment of student ability, but
also of teacher ability:

What supporters of this measure and even most of its
critics miss, however, is the debilitating effect of standardized testing on teachers. In the same way that teaching to the test requires less critical thinking by students,
teachers need not engage in critical thinking in order to
teach this material. In fact, teachers are actually being dis-
couraged from thinking for themselves. As curricula stan-
dardize around high-stakes exams, teachers become, in
essence, educational delivery systems rather than skilled
professionals. [Is Rees calling teachers the new conveyor
belt?] Consider the example of Edison Schools, Inc., [a
decade ago] the largest private company running public
schools in the United States. Edison likes to measure its
performance through state-standardized test scores. For
this reason, their curricula are highly standardized (75
percent is determined by the company and 25 percent
by local authorities). One Edison teacher told a reporter
for *Teacher Magazine* that 'independent-minded' teachers
might not be cut out to work for Edison. 'The program is
too rigid,' she says. This is one reason that a 'very high

percentage' of Edison teachers are at 'the beginning stages of their careers.' (Cookson, 2000)

With apologies to Mark Knofler, it looks like we've caught "Industrial Disease."

Rees points us still further:

> Another important methodological question raised by wholesale implementation of standardized testing comes from the field of history....If this method of educational assessment entirely takes over the education system, teachers who are trying to promote critical thinking rather than rote memorization will have to...teach more facts in lieu of greater critical analysis. Students will learn only dry, superficial facts *and the kind of teaching which inspires dedicated teachers to enter the historical profession will fall by the wayside.*...Bored students will become bored citizens with no understanding of where America has been and with no basis to judge where it is going in the future. (Rees 2001)

I wholeheartedly agree with Professor Rees's conclusion.

> If teachers cannot choose methods and topics that engage both them and their students, education will suffer. The reason for this is that contrary to the assumptions of standardized test advocates, education is not an ordinary commodity. It cannot accurately be measured in discreet units. Thus, it defies numerical measurement. Furthermore, there is no one best way to teach anything. Different content and different methods will work for different teachers in different settings. Destroying teacher prerogatives by introducing evaluation methods akin to scientific management will inevitably hurt production rather than help it along. (Rees 2001)

A corps of well-trained classroom professionals can more than adequately decide what techniques and methods to use to reach a wide variety of students, based on authentic and varied assessments.

Barry Schwartz of Swarthmore College writes and talks about "Practical Wisdom." It seems that with all the hoopla about education reform, and who is right about what it should look like, the powers that be simply keep overlooking practical wisdom: Do the right thing the right way for the right reason. It seems they are only concerned with who is right about deciding the right way. And, it seems, once getting the power to decide the right way, they set up ironclad rules to exclude other ways. This systemic approach also appeals to reformers because it is supposedly "foolproof." So, any teacher who can follow the model can do it. No tinkering, thinking, or practical wisdom required.

Detailed procedures or scripts are created to ensure that young, inexperienced teachers, more and more TFA recruited, will fit right into the "right" system's "right" way of doing education "right." These scripts also theoretically ensure that more experienced, poor, mediocre, fair, or even fairly good teachers get on board with the program the "right" way. However, what do these prescribed and proscribed scripts do to the very best creative and successful teachers who do not fit into the new "right"? Do they stop doing what worked extremely well? Do they stop using their practical wisdom?

According to Schwartz, one of the new, "right" ways is behavior modification, using incentives and negative sanctioning. They believe that, in our market-based, educational-reform scheme, self-interest (or selfishness) will get everyone to do the reformers' right things. So, we offer bonus pay for higher test scores and threaten job loss for lower test scores, as if the test scores on poorly designed tests actually matter as much as the market-based educators think.

Guess what? Psychologists know that doesn't work with kids or adults. They know it simply changes what is important to them. It changes the rules of the survival game. So, most teachers, being easily swayed by the incentives, simply stop helping kids learn and ensure they do well on the tests. These are not the same goals or achievements.

In a talk Schwartz did for TED.com, entitled "Using Our Practical Wisdom" (2010), he tells a story about Aristotle.

> Aristotle was very interested in watching how the craftsmen around him worked. And he was impressed at how they would improvise novel solutions to novel problems--problems that they hadn't anticipated. So, one example is, he sees these stonemasons working on the Isle of Lesbos, and they need to measure out round columns. Well, if you think about it, it's really hard to measure out round columns using a ruler. So what do they do? They fashion a novel solution to the problem. They created a ruler that bends, what we would call these days a tape measure--a flexible rule, a rule that bends. And Aristotle said, hah, they appreciated that sometimes to design rounded columns, you need to bend the rule. And Aristotle said often, in dealing with other people, we need to bend the rules.

The moral of this story is obvious. We need wise teachers, not scripted robots. As Schwartz put it in his TED talk, "A wise person knows when to improvise. And most important, a wise person does this improvising and rule-bending in the service of the right aims." It is true that too many new teachers come from the bottom ranks of classes (almost half from the bottom third). Why? The answers are simple. Pay and prestige. And as conditions worsen, who will choose this once-noble profession as a lifelong career? Very few.

SENIORITY, "BAD TEACHERS", AND TENURE

I keep reading the phrase, *toxic teachers*. It's a nice alliteration, but let's not be twisted by rhythmic rhetoric. Administrators very often know who the bad teachers are *before* granting them tenure, but are forced to grant it anyway because they have no alternatives. For years, especially in districts like New York City, principals literally have needed only a body in a room. For years, there was little hope of finding anyone better. Perhaps with more social conscience, greater respect, higher pay, and better working conditions more highly qualified college graduates will choose to teach--as they did in the 60s--for a variety of reasons. That explains the success of Finland. They have a far greater supply of highly qualified and career-pursuing candidates than the demand. If that happens here, the option of not granting tenure, as presently structured, is more realistic. Perhaps, with more districts doing a better job of training, and providing better professional development, mediocre teachers will become better. Perhaps, with better conditions and more trust, good teachers will stay longer, and the cycle of poor teachers will end.

That is a very controversial subject today. However, there is a lot of misinformation--what a surprise--about tenure and the role of unions in supporting tenure and the seniority-based system. If we did this as a lesson, we'd start with the following question:

Why were the seniority and tenure systems established in public school contracts? Unfortunately, our policy makers and media moguls ask it this way: Why are the seniority and tenure systems bad for our country? Who cries most and is heard most? It is the side that asks, as Bill Gates does, "Why does it take so long to fire bad teachers?"

Mayors and governors like New York City Mayor Bloomberg and New York State Governor Cuomo are seeking to establish themselves as powerful leaders by branding themselves as budget slashers. School leadership has become city or state budget management. Poll results rise and fall with their ability to say, "I got more done for less money," despite the fact that much less is getting done with less. Maybe they can run for President on that line. Younger teachers will resign before they are vested in the pension plan. That will lower costs. Average salaries will decrease, because the average age of teachers will drop to the late twenties or early thirties. Who would stay more than ten years? That will lower costs. In fact, this is already occurring. Median career length has decreased from fifteen to less than five years since 1990.

Is there any historical perspective? Our country is very proud of the First Amendment. Freedom of speech is what we, in theory, believe in as a foundation of the rights America stands for. Academic freedom is part of that first principle. In fact, seniority and tenure exist to protect that first principle from vindictive principals who had no problems firing teachers who might disagree with them or try innovative techniques or have children read *Huck Finn* or J.D. Salinger's *Catcher in the Rye*, or who might teach a class questioning Senator Joseph McCarthy. This happened regularly in this country. When teacher unions finally were established, they were not only established to try to pay teachers as professionals or give them the benefits that many other workers had for years, but also to protect them from the capriciousness of biased or prejudiced principals whose values and principles differed from teachers, regardless of how talented those teachers were. The unions (and the districts) simply agreed to a system that would include *due process* before firing.

Of course, we want the best teachers to teach our kids. But what happens when one of the best teachers in a school disagrees with a less talented administrator, who is less knowledgeable about actual teaching, or, as is true in many cases, callous and capricious. Without due process, that teacher is let go, fired, or suspended. What happens in school districts with no tenure, and the state slashes state aid? Who goes first? The most expensive is who. That practice, too is infecting this country. Using the euphemism "turn-around," school districts are encouraged to close bad schools by state governments, who, in turn, are bribed by the federal DOE money from Race to the Top. Told to rehire no more than 50 percent of the current staff and replace them with new people, districts slash labor costs that they couldn't do before. They also slash the education of their children, because most research shows that experience matters most in teaching.

Today, if I taught in a New York City high school under the new proposed system without due process, I would be fired for fighting against this new regime. Hundreds of good teachers, regardless of their superior talent and skill, have been relegated to ATR (Absent Teacher Reserve). There is a legitimate reason for due process. In a charter school, teachers can be easily let go for my differing opinion. Tenure needs reform, but it must continue to exist as due process. We should, as AFT president Randi Weingarten has pointed out, just change the name. Bad teachers need to be fired. Good teachers fired for the wrong reasons need to be protected. The common problem both sides have is that it takes too long, often years, for a case to be resolved. Both sides must be heard and a compromise reached. The Sixth Amendment helps answer the question,

"The accused shall enjoy the right to a speedy and public trial." Although the amendment refers to criminal trials, if we believe that the present, drawn-out process is criminal, we should fix it. There *are* bad teachers who *should* be let go. But institute a better method to streamline the "termination" process.

Seniority, not tenure, is the issue regarding reward and job security. Let's stop making tenure the issue. Once assured of due process, qualified supervisors must continuously evaluate their staff. But what does "qualified" mean? To me, that means only someone who is or has been a master teacher can judge another teacher. If hiring and firing are done by business-manager-style principals or district leaders, they must heed the advice of a teacher's immediate supervisor, and, if possible, a council of peers who know the situation best. Should student results be a part of the criteria? Yes, but not as presently devised. There is much work to be done to understand all the variables that go into measuring student success. The worst possible scenario is using unreliable, standardized test scores as the basis of these decisions. However, that is rapidly becoming a cancerous tumor spreading throughout states tied to Race to the Top money. Even worse than that would be the publicizing of these unscientific, inaccurate results being forced down the throats of schools and teachers by business-management leadership at the upper echelons of education. Yet, that is exactly what happened in New York City (a 2007-10 report was released in 2012) and Los Angeles (2011).

What are the intended and unintended consequences of these actions? The intended consequences are masked behind vitriolic attacks on unions and teachers. What are the costs? Ultimately, the opportunity costs in making these economic decisions will be students' lives. How can our leaders believe their own hype? How can so many Americans believe it? Are we that ignorant? Are we that naive? Maybe we didn't listen to the good teachers who taught us to *question* authority, not blindly follow it, like lemmings calmly walking off a cliff. Or walk right into Wendy Kopp's trap.

It is true that too many new teachers come from the bottom ranks of classes (almost half from the bottom third). Why? The answers are simple. Pay and prestige. And as conditions worsen, who will choose this once-noble profession as a lifelong career? Very few.

THE HYPE OF TFA

"Wendy Kopp proposed the idea for Teach For America in her Princeton Universityundergraduatethesis in 1989. In 1990, a charter corps of 500 committed recent college graduates joined Teach For America and began fueling the movement to eliminate educational inequity. Since then, nearly 33,000 participants have reached more than 3 million children nationwide during their two-year teaching commitments. They have sustained their commitment as alumni, working within education and across all sectors to help ensure that children growing up in low-income communities get an excellent education.

Given the magnitude of the achievement gap, we have aggressively worked to grow and deepen our impact. Our corps members and alumni have helped accelerate the pace of change as teachers, principals, elected officials, social entrepreneurs, and leaders in all fields. Alongside many others, they have proven that classrooms,schoolsand now whole communities can transform the life trajectories of all students, regardless of background.

We are energized by the progress we have made over the past 22 years and more hopeful than ever before that one day, all children in this nation will have the opportunity to attain an excellent education." (https://www.teachforamerica.org/our-organization/our-history)

That is how TFA defines itself. As a result of all the powerful endorsements and huge sums of money TFA has been granted, as its collective organizational ego grows, its collective head becomes bigger than its collective brain. To maintain the edge and power TFA has gained over the past decade, it constantly reinforces its newfound authority and power through very concrete means. It uses public media, who willingly feed the general public the TFA message. Politicians fall over themselves to get in line to congratulate TFA on its so called good work, with a photo op wherever possible.

To investigate TFA, let's start by following the money. The organization has grown rapidly since 1990, with nearly ten thousand Corps Members reaching more than five hundred thousand students. Its budget, funded by a mix of public and private sources, now approximates $300 million, including a recent $50 million grant garnered from the United States Department of Education. It is no coincidence that the same people who promote economic "freedom" and market forces--not equity--support TFA. They want to determine educational policy to gain profit. As Wendy D. Puriefoy (President of Public Education Network) stated, "The marketplace of education is a big market. There is a lot of *money* to be made." The best example is the Walton Family Foundation, based on the philanthropic beliefs of Wal-Mart founder Sam Walton. It is the single, largest contributor to Teach For America. Within the world of education foundations, Walton is synonymous with privatization and the promotion of vouchers for private schools.

Think. How many United States industries remain unexploited? To exploit the education industry, they are now doing what they have done to others: sidestep or crush unions; dissuade alternatives to their solutions (in our case, university programs); use the media to successfully sway the public to their side; and persuade politicians to do their bidding. If that doesn't work, TFA wants former CMs in positions of power. Leadership for Educational Equity (LEE) is a 501(c)(4) nonprofit organization that was launched in 2007 to inspire, train, and support Teach For America alumni and Corps Members to pursue public leadership by providing or connecting them to high-impact volunteer and career opportunities in politics, policy, advocacy, and elected office. In addition, TFA spends significant additional organizational time, energy, and money on its alumni--like Michelle Rhee, David Levin, and Mike Feinberg (founders of KIPP schools)--the source of the organization's true, political power.

"Temping" is a word I've been using to describe what school districts now seem to want to do, using budget crises and taxation issues as excuses, then making the changes permanent. They want to have a "temporary" corps of *unqualified* teachers who will last no longer than five years. They want to cut salary costs by decreasing the number of veteran teachers and replacing them with new teachers with a higher turnover rate within five years--and in TFA's case, two years.

Districts want to make more teachers quit prior to vesting in pensions to reduce long-term pension costs—even in times when there is no monetary crisis—as this pleases taxpayers. States are now pursuing this tactic to reduce their pension costs, as they push "teacher evaluation reform" and public disclosure of statistically unreliable and invalid ratings. TFA has convinced school districts to hire college grads who have read *Business Week*, in which TFA has been rated number seven in its top-ten listing of "The Best Places to Launch a Career." TFA's employment partners actively recruiting TFA alumni include: Goldman Sachs, JP Morgan, Credit Suisse, and Google. This may be good for some American corporate managers, but it is simply bad for American students.

Examples abound. In Washington, DC, former TFA Corps Member and former Schools Chancellor Michelle Rhee laid off 229 teachers, but only 6 of the 170 TFA teachers in the system. In Boston, the district planned to lay off 20 veteran teachers and replace them with TFA Corps Members, until the union filed a complaint. Boston Teachers Union President Richard Stutman met with eighteen local union presidents, "all of whom said they'd seen teachers laid off to make room for TFA members," according to an article in *USA Today*.

In the Charlotte-Mecklenburg district, for instance, the superintendent laid off hundreds of veteran teachers, but spared 100 TFA CMs. TFA, meanwhile, expanded into Dallas, bringing in nearly 100 new teachers, even though the district had laid off 350 teachers in the 2008-09 school year.

In Huntsville, Alabama, even with research showing its flaws, TFA was hired via a $1.7 million contract to provide 170 teachers over the next four years. However, the contract will be reviewed every year, so if the TFA teachers do not provide results, the Board of Education can cancel the contract.

Montgomery, Alabama is replacing fired veteran teachers with young teachers from TFA. And in Detroit, the local education authority plans to bring in 200 Teach For America Corps Members after nearly a score of

Detroit public schools were closed and hundreds of veteran teachers let go. TFA has proposed to start all TFA schools to replace some of those closed schools. TFA's current labor policies--which turn it into a source of "replacement labor"--place it beyond the scope of education reform and into the realm of *union* busting. Was that its original plan? It seems to be now. What has their growing power and prestige produced? Why do we stand for it?

I taught high school economics for years. What we buy with our limited resources comes down to the laws of supply and demand, scarcity of resources, opportunity costs, and the values we use to decide what we would rather have. What we give up to get what we want more are our *opportunity costs*. For a student, the question may be, Do I want to go to the concert? I may have to forgo studying for that test. If I want to do well on that test, I may have to forgo that concert. In this case, the resource is time. The decision will be based on what the student values more. Will it be time spent on entertainment or education?

For most school districts, the public determines how to spend the resource of money. The public tells the districts they want lower taxes. The public says teachers are good people, just overpaid and under-worked. They are, perhaps, envious of the pension plans our unions have fought for. They think anyone can teach, even TFA novices right out of college with no training. Yet, the public also wants better education. Economically, their demand for lower education costs makes better education the unfortunate opportunity cost. That is backward.

However, if the public tells district school boards they no longer want the seemingly less expensive education TFA and others are selling, and, in fact, demands better education and a way to really attract the best teachers, boards will have to listen and react, or be voted out of office. This, in fact, is what makes districts like Scarsdale successful. Over the years, it has attracted scores of extremely talented teachers from neighboring districts, including New York City, because of better salary and benefits, respect, and a professional attitude toward teacher training, professional development, and new-teacher mentoring.

Let's focus on TFA myths. A close look at TFA retention rates tells us a different story than what TFA wants us to believe. Peer-review studies on the efficacy of new TFA CMs also tells an inconvenient truth. Interviews with CMs done by journalists, educators like me, or researchers have found a much different story than what the TFA Kool-Aid provides.

First, a look at TFA's website indicates how they distort the truth. TFA implies that 67 percent of Corp Members stay in education after two years. However, here is the truth. By looking at TFA's own data, we actually find that of that 67 percent who "stay in education," only 52 percent teach K-12. Of that 52 percent, only 58 percent teach in *public* schools. That equates to approximately 20 percent actually teaching in public schools after their two years are completed. That 20 percent retention rate is a far cry from the 67 percent they mislead the public into believing are actually retained. It also creates havoc in schools desperately trying to gain some sort of staff stability, a key factor in any school's success.

Using TFA's own data, let's see where all the other *so-called* educators are.

- 32% go on to work for TFA

- 18% become some level of district or school leader after two years

- 18% go back to grad school [1]

- 15% become what is called "school-based professionals"

- 9% join other policy groups, like E4E or Students First

- 6% become district or Charter Management Organization administrators

- These are not exactly teaching positions. Recently, a colleague, Professor Mark Naison of Fordham University noted that, "some of the nation's top law schools are offering 50 percent scholarships for Teach For America Corps Members! So much for promoting teaching as a lifetime career!"

Teach For America also boasts about its impact on education and academic achievement, noting on its webpage: "[O]ur Corps Members and alumni work relentlessly to increase academic achievement." Yet, in a

---

1

"*Mathematica*" study touted by TFA, "the students of Corps Members remained far below their national peers and made only marginal gains."

The study, using the Iowa Test of Basic Skills, also showed that neither the TFA group nor the control group (teachers who taught in the same schools and in the same grade levels, but with "substantially lower rates of certification and formal education training" than a nationally representative sample of teachers) was even beginning to close the achievement gap. According to Dr. Phillip Kovacs (University of Alabama, Huntsville), peer-reviewed research over the past ten years continually points out the fact that, "students of TFA teachers did not perform significantly different from students of other undercertified teachers, and that students of certified teachers outperformed students of teachers who were undercertified."

> This inequitable distribution of effective teachers further
> compounds the disadvantage that high-poverty and high-
> minority students are faced with in school. Children most
> in need of strong teachers are being denied what arguably
> might be their most invaluable resource--teachers, which
> is reinforcing the inequalities. (Vasquez Heilig, J., Cole,
> H. and Springel, M. 2011).

Why there are so few peer-reviewed studies looking at TFA is a more interesting question. Perhaps it is because TFA doesn't want them. Discussing why TFA doesn't release information on how its Corps Members perform, CEO and founder Wendy Kopp was rather candid, "We just don't feel it's responsible to show," Kopp said. "There are so many flaws in our system."

How TFA can continue to make the claim that they produce Corps Members who make "as much of an impact on student achievement as veteran teachers" despite evidence to the contrary is a fairly simple matter. It comes back to money and power. Thanks to massive grants and payments from school districts around the country, TFA can afford a massive public-relations campaign that includes directly lobbying the federal government. *We need to outdo that lobbying effort.*

There is a great deal of information circulating about TFA's soft under-belly, but it is not public. These truths must come out before it is too late. Where is Michael Moore? Barbara Veltri (*Learning on Other People's Kids: Becoming a Teach For America Teacher*) and I have proposed a film whose purpose is not simply to shed light on the underside of TFA in real schools, but to face real questions in education and provide solutions. This film seeks to be about how poorly we are doing in providing the kind of teaching professionals who are in teaching as a career, not a 'community service project.'

The purpose of this film is to show the dichotomies between TFA-trained teaching and successful teaching. It seeks to show the error in the thought that teachers are made, not born: that any smart person can teach. The purpose of this film is to show how the concepts of Frederick Winslow Taylor's 'Scientific Management' of the early twentieth century are being used again in the twenty-first in a modern version of corporate control over labor.

The purpose is to show how now, as then, the children of rich and powerful leaders go to private schools and are taught by powerfully creative teachers, while the millions of poor, toiling (future) workers are taught by step-by-step automatons who pass down and enforce the menial skills 'needed' by the 'unthinking' masses. The purpose is to [show] how poor kids are being told they are being taught to be future leaders. The reality is that how they are being taught does no such thing.

Ultimately, we are here about how we can educate all of our kids, regardless of their socioeconomic strata, if we stop believing the hype. Instead of hype, we need solutions. School districts must make better decisions. We must force our *school districts* to force TFA to change. If districts don't hire TFA and its CMs, TFA must either adapt or die.

Districts must hire credentialed, new teachers who have had sufficient teacher training and student teaching internships. Districts should only use Teach For America staffing when there is both a shortage of qualified teachers and the alternative is to hire other uncertified and emergency teachers or substitutes. Districts should not assign TFAs to teach special education classes; CMs are not skilled in general education, let alone, SPED law and issues of remediation. Districts should not request or require TFAs to write grants, tutor kids after school, coach, sponsor clubs, or assume 'extra' duties during their first year. They are trying to figure out teaching, and that alone consumes their time.

The public must resolve to take action. They must go to board meetings and make demands to end this craziness called 'reform.' They must and can demand that districts and TFA work together with universities to provide committed, well-trained teachers. They must and can tell school boards:

TFA must be forced to provide schools with people who see teaching as a career, not just a stepping-stone or an altruistic act of community service. TFA and school district financial managers can find a way to co-finance this. A true, financial partnership can and must be arranged to develop career teachers. [Use] the $70,000 that districts pay for two-year CMs to train and support a new teacher more dedicated to teaching as a career. Districts can pay CMs jointly. The $5,000 (finder's fee) that districts pay to TFA can be used to hire cadres of effective veteran teachers to 'coach the Corps' on-site. All districts must provide a dedicated mentor program with veteran teachers or field specialists who want to mentor Corps Members and all new teachers, and have this duty as their full-time job. Top-flight districts and private schools already do this successfully.

The inadequate, five-week TFA institute must be replaced by a teamed approach with universities to design a longer MAT program specifically for Corps members and their realities and to create career teachers. The first year of that MAT plan must be composed of training, student teaching, substitute teaching, and being paired up as an assistant to a veteran teacher or more experienced Corps Member. As a result, second-year CMs would have the benefit of getting assistance from the incoming, first-year CMs. *No* graduate classes should be taken the first year. First-year teaching is far too rough as it is.

CMs need more "do this tomorrow," and less theory in the beginning of this MAT program and to value the expertise of instructors who are experienced practitioners of the socioeconomic, grade levels, and subject realities that TFAs are dealing with. New CMs and other new teachers must learn different, creative, and interesting teaching and classroom management strategies for all types of students. More focus should also be given to learning about child development, child psychology, and sub-cultural pedagogy. One size does *not* fit all.

Above all, school boards must be forced to understand the commitment by TFA recruits should be to make teaching a career, not a stopover.

TFA claims it did a study and that a longer commitment would scare away many of their top applicants. That's fine. We only want those who will commit to teaching. We want this to be a part of an overall commitment to developing career teachers, as we do career lawyers. Check the Finnish model. It can be done.

TFA will never give in, you say? Exactly. This will be hard to do, because TFA is extremely attached to its power, its long-range plan to dominate and influence policy, and its diabolical plan to further achieve those ends. Although the leadership of TFA is closely allied with forces seeking to privatize public education, and use high-stakes testing as a vehicle to rate teachers and administrators, there are many TFA Corps Members, past and present, who believe that racism, and poverty, are the primary causes of neighborhood distressand economic stagnationin the United States.

It is time that these people, who now number in the thousands, organize a progressive caucus in TFA to fight within the organization to reduce its emphasis on high-stakes testing, encourage TFA Corps Members to make teaching their lifetime career, and have TFA openly join with veteran teachers and universities to actively improve teacher training in America. A concerted effort by students, teachers, parents, school districts, and universities can make this happen. Let's use their own rhetoric to force them to change. TFA reformers like to say that we have to stop doing what is good for the adults and start doing what is good for the kids. A long-range plan to develop more career teachers would be better for the kids. Remember the kids.

TFA leadership is driving federal policy to abandon preparation requirements altogether. We all need to push back to ensure that teacher quality means equitable distribution of fully prepared and effective teachers. The *goals* are simple: Prepare well-trained, career teachers who will not be scripted by TFA, and return education to the professionally trained, experienced educators who have studied and practicedand mastered the art and science of teaching.

Barbara Tuchman, in her 1984 book, *The March of Folly, from Troy to Vietnam,* defines *folly* asthe "pursuit of public policy contrary to self-interest, where people pursue the same failed policies and expect different results." What better example of *folly* is there than current public education policy? When there is enough demand by teachers, not just the unions; by students, not just the usual demonstrators; by administrators, more than in school administrators; and by parents, a *majority*, to stop the nonsense imposed by ignorant (about education) legislators and governors and their corporate goons (including TFA), then we can get back to finding enough real teachers to do real teaching. We need to stop the squabbling among ourselves. As long as TFA is still with us, we must get it to change and reform.

However, we cannot do that by simply protesting, blogging, and parading. We must bring political power back to the hands of the people. In most places in this country, the last vestige of real democracy is in education. Citizens not only elect school board members, they vote on budgets. They control what school boards decide. They can create a fabulous public education in their own district. The bigger concern is in cities where citizens have relinquished that power to mayoral-controlled Departments of Education, as in New York City, where Mayor Bloomberg has allied with the education forces of evil and their corporate allies to conduct education as a business. However, even in the cases of larger cities, or states, unhappy citizens can make a change. I firmly believe if districts were forced by the public to stop hiring TFA in its current form and, instead, demanded TFA reforms, then the laws of supply and demand would take hold. TFA either adapts or dies.

My work allowed me to mentor Teach For Americans in a major urban area. The young men and women I work with are wonderful, bright, and motivated to do the best job they can, but they are both woefully unprepared by a five-week, crash course and generally unsupported by the supervisors from TFA and those in their schools. Too often, they are thrown into classrooms and "supervised" by people who cannot teach them how to teach, because they don't know how.

In most cases, they are not being taught the art of teaching; they are being "taught" how to "class manage" and train their students, as if they were trainable animals, not thinking and capable human beings. The first time they hear that class management is the result of good teaching, not the other way around, is when they hear it from me. Unfortunately, in most of the schools TFA cohorts are placed in, class management and test preparation have become the means and end to provide students with the tools to minimally pass standardized tests.

Teaching is more than preparing students for standardized tests. In fact, teaching done well always prepared students for a variety of tests, including problem-solving and critical-thinking tests. We all know who our best teachers were. They inspired us to learn, and, often, we didn't even realize how much we learned. We know what worked and what made us curious and what made us thoughtful, human learners.

I am amazed at what TFA and the so-called educators in these schools are forcing my Teach For America Corps Members to do. As a master teacher for thirty-eight years in three different high schools, I have collected a variety of techniques: some my own, and some borrowed from nationally known colleagues who students held in great respect. With one exception, I have yet to see these proven artistic and mechanical techniques exhibited or taught to my small group. Here is what I have discovered: My Corps Members got little to no support. They are told what to do, but not how. In one young lady's case, there was not a face-to-face conversation about teaching with a supervisor until November, after I first saw her.

My boss was right. These courageous, first-year teachers are put under horrendous stress. They have no time to do anything but learn to survive and make it to the next day. The e-mails I got from them were often addressed at 4:00 am, yes, 4:00 am, because of all of the nonteaching work they are forced to do on top of the real work of planning, assessing, and providing feedback.

There was little quality teaching going on. They saw the value of what outsiders like me give, but are afraid to use it, or they will be accused of not following the rules the school has set for them. When I asked if it would help for me to talk to their assistant principals (APs) or supervisors, they decline. They are afraid, especially if their immediate supervisor is a TFA-trained person. This is very different from those schools where I have had great chats with principals and APs who are open to a myriad of ideas and are not ideological missionaries.

My first-year Corps Members talked to me about trying to make their kids responsible for their work and training them to learn skills, such as taking and organizing notes, but it doesn't fit the lesson plan structure they are given. As a result, one receives warnings and Us. I have watched one young female Corps Member, and with proper training, she--as all of my TFAs--can and will be good teachers, but not under the conditions they work in now, and using the types of planning and assessing they are being told to use. That is the shame of TFA.

John B. was a TFA corps member mentee of mine who quit. In January of 2013, John returned from Afghanistan to serve our nation as a member of the New Jersey National Guard. He wrote this in his first letter to me on his way to Afghanistan,

> It is not whether or not we are afraid, but what we do with that fear today. We are all afraid right now: of the future, for our profession, for our students. But that shall not stop us from linking arms, not just with one another, but with parents, children, and administrators. It shall not stop us from fighting the sinister and cynical alliance between government, corporations, and individuals They may have money, power, and influence; but what they do not have a monopoly on is what remains hidden in the human heart.

> We understand this. We know that we are not factory workers, and that our children are not cogs. Our lives are joined, and they progress in the rhythms of joy and sadness and love and anxiety that propel their young hearts and minds forward. They are smart; they question; and they hunger for something beyond a test question. They are names and faces and stories: the quiet bravery of a boy who never missed a day of school despite facing the upheavals of the city foster care system; the learning-disabled girl who flipped diligently between textbook and dictionary every day, trying so hard to make sense of the words on the page. We are privy to the small triumphs that renew a child's world; we know the power of knowledge and the thrill of seeking it. Those who would seek to cheapen or dismiss such moments as untestable miss the point of the profession, as well as its strength.

The journey ahead will be long and challenging and marked by the minor victories and stinging defeats that so many of us know from our lives in the classroom. It will not be a season of rewards, nor will it be one of redemption; instead, it will be one of progression. We will fight them at the ballot boxes, and with our words, and with our protests; we will fight them with all the dignity that our profession demands from us. We cannot know whether or not it is too late. We simply must believe that it is not.

Most showed good potential. A couple showed great potential. Two really excelled; interesting that they were both in the same really well-run high school. One stayed to teach; the other went off to medical school.

It hurt to see my first- and second-year Corps Members so unhappy in a job they should feel joyous about. It hurts to read disparaging remarks about my profession. It hurts to see friends want to retire sooner than need be because of increased testing and policy that do not improve teaching and learning. It hurts that so many high-qualified experts, who teach, are not heard. And it peeves me that the policy makers are letting the highest bidders determine policy, all in the name of reform.

I looked at the published New York City Teacher Report Cards for the year 2009-10. Of my nineteen TFA CMs, only four were listed. One who I found to have great potential (and, in fact, is still teaching in his fifth year) received a 40. Another with fabulous potential, now in her fourth year, received two ratings–for separate classes in the same school. Her ratings were 8 and 84. If you think that was odd, consider another who rated 31 as an ELA teacher and 80 as a math teacher. She was hired to teach social studies. Here are their responses to those ratings:

I was a little confused by the ratings. At my school, the same teacher was in the 3rd percentile for sixth grade and the 93rd for seventh. Huh? I think it's because she teaches a Special Ed bridge class, so her percentages probably fluctuate wildly, depending on the two sixth-graders or so she has in a given year, but still.

I think the entire thing is ridiculous, but what can we do? Personally, my data is extremely skewed. I had five kids on my report (who scored very poorly) who I never even taught, and two additional kids who were out of my room for the majority of the year for suspensions. They made up almost 25 percent of my data. Also, I taught about 50 percent ELL students, 25 percent Special Ed., and we all know that if students can't read on grade level, they surely can't pass the ELA or math tests.

I can speak for many of my colleagues when I say that honestly, we just feel like punching bags at this point. What's another shot? Every night, when I sit doing hours of work at home, I think, what's the point? I love the kids and that's why I'll continue working as hard as I can, but eventually that just won't be enough. I never thought that day would come, but after the last few months, I just can't find much incentive to being a teacher anymore.

The data reports weren't an issue for any of us today, whether they were good or bad. We know how hard we work, and the kids who want to work and the parents who push them to do so *are* learning in our classrooms. Thanks for the continued support.

Using my first name is fine. I think what is most frustrating to me is that, over halfway through my fourth year, I finally feel like I'm coming into my own as a teacher. Sure, I was a good teacher my first few years (after those awful first few months!) but now is when a lot of us from 2008 feel like we're starting (very early stages!) to become great teachers. Most people I've talked to say that it takes about five years or so to feel this, and I think by next year I will be completely over the 'new teacher' hurdle, at least in my own mind. So, it's a shame that this is when being a teacher is becoming increasingly more difficult. I guess we'll see what the future holds, but I don't foresee [UFT president] Mulgrew being able to rally the troops to make any type of significant change for us as a group of professionals. But I'm not taking the glass half-full just yet!

They did not want their names revealed.

I did not spend enough time with my CMs. Fordham required me to visit with them ten times in their first year and four times in their second. They need me (or someone like me) everyday, preferably an experienced master teacher to act as a mentor. They are too stressed to call or meet with me outside the frantic hours they already keep. What they really needed was to be trained in a manner that would have prepared them for the hardest job they could have imagined, not the hype fed to them by TFA during recruiting.

THE PAIN OF TFA

It's 8:30 am in a middle school classroom in the South Bronx, about a quarter of a mile from where I spent my teenage years. R., a second-year TFA Corps Member and I are in her classroom talking about her plans for the next period. We expect the kids to come up any second and get started. Suddenly, two kids push open the doors panting, trying to catch their breath. R. and I, figuring they were just being normal, unruly thirteen-year-olds, ask them why they are running. They tell us of the shooting in a park about half a block away where kids congregate before they enter the school. Then they sit, and a couple of minutes later the class begins. After class, R. tells me how scared she was and how her heart was racing uncontrollably for the entire class. She is amazed at her kids' calm. R. is from upper-middle-class, suburban, South Florida.

I have seen their tears, fears, anxieties, and heartaches. I have seen their moments of joys, successes, and achievements. Unfortunately, the latter are far fewer. Educators who work with these young people often are confused about TFA and its motives, procedures, and effectiveness. Often, they question the motivation of the participants. I have heard people accuse them of using their TFA experience only to pad applications to future graduate study or careers. I am sure for some that is true. For most of these kids--and please don't forget, they are kids--it's a rather painful way to get into grad school. The road is hard. It is filled with potholes the size of canyons.

Barbara Veltri in her book, *Learning on Other People's Kids: Becoming a Teach For America Teacher*) relates J.'s story. "One morning, in the second month of school, a fifth-grade girl is outside my classroom, crying with family members: Her big brother was shot by the police a few hours before. I was just out of "Institute," and I had no bag of tricks. How did I know what to do?"

Teach For America is not a monolith. Of the nineteen corps members I personally have worked with, several were quite good. A few have stayed and are now in their fourth and fifth year, and have told me they want to continue. I hope so. Many Corps Members are hardworking, thoughtful, and even radical. Few CMs quit--about 9-10 percent--but more want to. Former TFA CM (1991) and now a TFA critic and blogger, Gary Rubenstein, said, "Really, there were only two things that kept me from quitting. One was based on luck — I had such great friends that helped me get through it. We'd get to school at 6:30 am and leave at 6:00 pm, so the four or so hours that I was actually in front of a class was only about 33 percent of my day. The rest of the time, we planned a little, but mostly just traded war stories and laughed a lot about our situation. The other thing that kept me in the classroom was that I really didn't have any 'Plan B' — there was no deferred law school acceptance or anything like that."

John B. was going to be a good teacher. He had the instincts. He had the talent. He did not have the training or support. Here are some excerpts from his e-mailed explanation to me. (I have inserted blanks to maintain the anonymity of the school and school personnel.)

- I went into TFA with a realistic perspective on the difficulties ahead; what I did not expect was the kind of managerial incoherence and lack of structure that has become a hallmark of my time at ------. My experiences have led me to disagree with TFA's model of placing inexperienced and idealistic teachers (many of whom come from entirely different worlds than their students) in the classrooms of these institutions, many of which have been dysfunctional for a generation or longer, and expecting them to be successful. Given my post-Institute experiences, it no longer makes any sense to me (not to mention that Institute itself was a highly structured and supported psychological booster that provided very little in the way of training or preparation for these schools).

- I have been placed in a school with no books, no curriculum, and a set of administrators whose schizophrenic responses to issues of communication and discipline have reflected leadership at its worst. I have known poor leaders, and I have served with some whose own personal shortcomings have limited their ability to get out in front and set a proper example, but never have I seen such shameful and disgraceful leadership as I have seen at this school.

- ...--- -------, the assistant principal from -------- --------, once informed me in front of a colleague that my classroom was 'out of control' without providing any positive next steps; another time, she asked me if my children were 'always...talking' after a brief informal observation, then provided no further instruction nor contact.

- ---- -----, (The 'Executive Principal') bullies and intimidates the children; for example, the other day he walked into my classroom with two armed police officers, both of whom were wearing their side arms, and pulled out two girls who were standing up and looking out the window. Once outside, the officers spoke in intimidating tones to the two girls, demanding that they look at them when they speak, take their hands out of their pockets, and asking them if they needed classes in how to respect adults. The grotesque implications of two police officers interrogating children of color in such a way while ----- looked on (and told the children that they, the typical troublemakers, would no longer be allowed to do what they wanted to) shocked and offended me. It also reflected the kind of disturbing incoherence that has marked the school's disciplinary response-- after doing virtually nothing besides yelling at children for six months ---- went to a kind of nuclear option, and the suggestion of side arms (which normal school safety officers do not wear, I have noted) implies that violence will be visited upon the children. Such power should only be reserved for the worst fights, threats, or brandishing of weapons.

- The work environment that he creates is no better; he expects new teachers to arrive at his forty-five-minute long 'New Teacher Support Group' on Thursday mornings, which one day consisted of him telling us to come up with lists of items to ask for on 'Donors Choose.' Another day, an AP asked us to differentiate passages from a health textbook. None of us are health teachers. Furthermore, as new teachers, we need our prep time (as I am sure you remember), and such a waste of our time is disrespectful to us, and surely only fulfills some statistical need for PD [Personal Development].

- Five out of six first-year teachers (including myself) and one second-year teacher have been given unsatisfactory ratings on their formal observations, a pattern which, when paired with other administrative behaviors toward teachers, suggests that the administrators understand that the school is a sinking ship and are gaming a plan to place the blame squarely upon the teachers, so that they may fly away and alight upon another six-figure salary somewhere else.

- In my case, I received a U because my consequence ladder was unclear; there was very little comment on the actual substance of the lesson, and the AP mistitled the lesson in the formal observation paperwork as a conclusions writing workshop when it was actually introductions. A later, informal observation showed similar issues of inattention; the AP wrote down that there were multiple side conversations without remarking upon my use of a consequence ladder, my handling of an argument between two students, and the fact that I moved the seat of one of the girls to where my laptop was so that she could properly see the photos she had to write about (she is legally blind). He also remarked that he was confused when I said that we were 'switching to fiction,' when I had, in fact, said, 'we are switching to captions,' which made sense, because we were looking at photos and writing captions.

- I have given my all, and I am angry, disillusioned, and unful-filled. I have spent hours preparing and planning, only to have things washed away by the dysfunctional and undisciplined nature of this school.

- I have come up with points and incentive systems only to have the children lose anydeeply rooted sense of investment. I have spent thousands of my own dollars making photocopies and buying supplies and rewarding good behavior. I begged, bor-rowed, and asked for my own literature textbooks from friends and family members to supplement my own curriculum. I held my own detention before the advent of the school's After School Academy in an attempt to assert my own authority. I sent students to the Dean and Grade Team Leaders, only to be-come more confused and inhibited by their responses, which told me that I was not asserting my authority. I averaged three to four parents a night in phone calls, only to have troubled children improve for a period (if at all) and then fall back into their destructive habits.

- The best support was what I received from my Fordham men-tor, who actually gave me the substance of teaching and helped me understand the dynamics in my classroom and work with the children to our mutual advantage.

- If I stay here, I will be a piece of the systemic dysfunction that plagues this school. TFA has a moral obligation to not place teachers in schools [as poorly run] like this one; if not for the good of these children, then for the good of future generations who may benefit from teachers who are brought up in profes-sional, supportive environments that provide the structures necessary for children and adults to thrive--teachers who will be retained because of their satisfaction with what they do and who they are.

(A note. John went back to school full time. He wrote his masters degree in history. He finished his master's thesis entitled, "The Crisis of Competency: How New York City's Fiscal Crisis Contributed to the Decline of Its School System, 1970–-1980.")

One of my biggest frustrations for new teachers--TFA or otherwise--is not only the lack of quality time to prepare to teach, but also, more significantly, the lack of highly qualified mentors to train them. In my work with nineteen first- and second-year TFA Corps Members I was both encouraged and shocked by the large number of younger teachers in their schools. Don't get me wrong, I love the energy they bring, but, oh, the inexperience! Too often, novices trained novices in how to follow the simple, prescribed scripts TFA or their school "leaders" gave them, while prohibiting techniques more experienced teachers know work. It often became my job to find a compromise between what they were being told to do, and what seasoned experienced professionals know works to improve how and what students learned as opposed to "increase student test scores."

TFA Corps Members are doomed unless they can wean themselves off of the prescribed formulas. That is not likely to happen for two reasons: TFA puts a lot of pressure on them to do it the TFA way; they also give you the big TFA teat to suckle. TFA becomes like an enabling parent. As a result, only the strong and more independent types of TFA Corps Members will wean themselves from TFA. That is more likely to happen with a mentor who knows about, and successfully uses, alternative methods.

Unfortunately, many mentors are also still inhibited either by policies, TFA, or other big, approved programs. The Teachers College Workshop model comes to mind. By the way, early in 2013, even the New York City Department of Education realized that model didn't work. Mentors and more experienced teachers must change as well. They must recognize that there is more than one way kids learn. They must become students of teaching, so that they can pass along what they discover to the people they mentor. When did teachers, especially mentors of new teachers, stop becoming students themselves?

The next issue that creates so much difficulty for TFA Corps Members is that the schools they teach in vary. Some have administrators and staff that welcome quality teaching and are not locked in to "teach to the test" agenda-based lessons, and the like. They run more professional cultures where teachers can innovate and use ideas in their planning, such as culturally responsive pedagogy. However, they are the minority. Most schools have overbearing administrators who force non-experienced corps members to rely on TFA materials and other corporate prepared materials or lose their jobs. These "school leaders" aren't teacher mentors as mine were; many have never even taught.

Remember, these TFA corps members are very young. In today's society, it simply takes longer to become a mature adult. Although successful as students, many TFA kids are naïve. They are idealistic, and often followers. They were great students because they learned to obey the authorities in their schools, follow directions, behave well, and do as they were told. They are perfect fodder for TFA and authoritarian administrators.

Will prospective TFA Corps Members be willing to add extra time to their "commitment" to teaching, or are too many not really interested in teaching as a career enough to sacrifice that extra semester or year of training? Will TFA accept a longer commitment of time as well as non TFA staff teachers and techniques? Unfortunately, I think not. Wendy Kopp and her TFA (the organization) have become more and more like an empress with no clothes. As it gains more and more corporate and political supporters and funding, TFA is less inclined to do the kind of self evaluation good teachers and good schools do.

Who among the TFA courtiers will tell the empress the truth? Arne Duncan? No. President Obama? No. Who will be so bold as to say, "Wendy, you did a good thing getting so many new and able people to be at least interested in teaching. But now, what are you going to do to make things better?"

How will you:

- decrease the number of resume builders who join the corps and leave after two years for the *ivy* grad school or Goldman Sachs?

- decrease the number of TFA CMs who idealistically want to do two years of peace corps but are afraid to go to Africa?

- decrease the number of "teacherpreneurs" who enter the corps to do their two years and go on to the new, "for-profit" educational world?

- decrease the number of TFA CMs who see the administrative or business end of TFA as their life's work, not teaching?

- decrease the number of hardworking and sincere TFA CMs who drop out because they find themselves unprepared to start and undersupervised for their two-year stint?

Finally, how will you increase the number of well-prepared, well-supervised, professional teachers for whom teaching is a long term profession, not a stepping stone; who seek advice, constructive criticism, peer review, and cooperation from experienced people outside the "Chosen"?

Teach For America describes itself as a "national corps of outstanding, recent college graduates of all academic majors and career interests who commit two years to teach in urban and rural public schools and become leaders in the effort to expand educational opportunity." TFA has indoctrinated its recruits to believe that what they give them is Godlike. TFA has always had a peace corps image. To some extent, that is a good thing. I am in favor of more community service work before embarking on a career. But sometimes, that ideal turns into missionary zeal, and the idea that a particular service organization has the only answers.

Veltri tells us that most TFA Corps Members do not have command of the 4 Cs: culture of schools, culture of community, culture of curriculum, and culture of classroom management. Most lack the practical wisdom or street smarts to have a good chance of success in the schools where they are placed. Most Corp Members are successful, young college students with no experience, and with usually no desire to teach long-term. Although successful as students, many TFA kids are naïve. They are idealistic, and often followers. They are perfect fodder for TFA leaders. They are taught by TFA to follow. Stay in line. Be formulaic. Do not be like those older teachers: wise, creative, independent, and spontaneous. Most of all, they are trained by TFA to be a Corps Member above all, and not a part of a school or district. How much does the public know about what TFA does *to* its CMs--as opposed to *for* them--once a district hires them? TFA "supervisors" --formerly called PDs (Program Directors), now called MTLDs (Managers of Teacher Leadership)--with only two years experience come into Corps Members' schools to reinforce the TFA data-driven gospel, and tell Corps Members they must rely on TFA-prepared materials to be successful. Few of my kids tell me they have any relationship with their MTLDs. Only one tells me she has actually relied on hers. In addition, once at a school, and on top of the time they spend teaching, they must attend mandatory TFA meetings at TFA headquarters.

I can't tell you how painful it was to watch so many young people cry to me because of the pressure put on them by TFA to do all of these things. In some cases, CMs actually travel hours out of their way to go to a local TFA headquarters, because they feel they must go to a meeting or get the already prepared materials to copy and plug into the prescribed curriculum. The end result is submitting them to more TFA "Kool-Aid" and discouraging them from trying other things that might actually work.

In fact, because of all the assessment forms they must fill out, and the other time-consuming, anti-teaching TFA rituals, not only don't they have the time to accurately assess their 130 students as TFA would like, they can't even devote the time to good lesson planning, so they use TFA-provided worksheets, cookie-cutter, "teacher-proof," formulaic, guided-worksheet lesson plans. Many CMs see the value of the teaching materials non-TFA trainers and supervisors provide, but are afraid to use them, because they will be accused of not following TFA rules and lose their stipends.

The recurring theme recanted to me over and over by almost all of my CM mentees is that TFA is not only of little help, but it puts even more stress on them than they already incur, being untrained novices working under the most difficult of conditions. In fact, they have told me TFA does not teach them to work smarter. Nor does TFA teach them to how to organize their time and workload. It does not even really teach questioning technique, or many of the most important tools a quality teacher needs to succeed. Stuck in quicksand up to their nostrils while being between the proverbial rock and hard place, most CMs find it difficult to take the rope (advice) from an outside mentor, even when they know the rope can save them. They often let go, only to become more frustrated and filled with self-doubt, remorse, and the goal of getting out after their two-year sentence is up. All of this is in addition to what any new teacher in a school in a high-poverty area must face.

There are thousands of TFA Corps Members who have a different story to tell than what TFA is passing off as the truth. The TFA Institute simply does not prepare them. CMs are told fairy tales about their superiority. CMs are told to think like a "Corps Member." CMs are given empty slogans, not practical wisdom. "Work it, work it, work it." "Every child is a leader."

CHAPTER 3:

DO THE RIGHT THINGS RIGHT

LET'S ASSESS NOT TEST

Regarding data. There is a huge difference between being data driven and data guided. Assessments of all types, not just fill-in-the-bubble, multiple-choice tests, must be analyzed to see how students progress with particular skills of various levels and content. Essays, projects, group projects, research, and class participation are all assessment, as well as teaching tools. They used by teachers and their students for self-assessment. Teachers are only as good as their students understanding of how good they are.

Good teachers constantly reassess methods and assessments. Are they appropriate for those kids? Are they challenging without being too hard? They better not be too easy. That is condescending. Is there clear linkage between your objectives, outcomes, goals, methods, questions, and assessments? Do the students understand why they are doing what they are doing, as well as what to do and how? That is also important. Are the assessments too hard? Are they too easy? Are they assessing the wrong things? Are they authentically assessing what they should? Do they match the lessons? Do the lessons match them? Do you remember Mel Brooks as the 2000-year old teacher with the 1000-year-old yellow and crinkly plans? You probably don't, except for that, and the ability to steal or copy old papers and tests from older friends and family members.

What is assessment? That depends on whom you ask. When I was a kid in school, we were never assessed. We were tested. We took in-class tests, IQ tests, and entrance tests to specialized high schools, and, of course, those other standardized tests: the New York State Regents and SATs. I taught for over twenty years before I was introduced to the term "assessment," when I first heard Grant Wiggins speak about "Authentic Assessment." "Holy Cow," I exclaimed, "I didn't know I had been doing that for so many years." Ever since I started teaching, I was trained to "assess" how my students were doing at reaching the outcomes I had laid out for them. Teachers, need to know if students have gotten the "its" of the lesson then let their students know if they have or haven't. Additionally, we must have the means to give them the best feedback, to either tell them they have it, or that they don't. Most importantly, if they don't have it, our feedback, based on the results of the use of authentic assessments, must tell them how to get it.

In a September 19, 2010 op-ed piece in *The New York Times* entitled "Scientifically Tested Tests," Susan Engel of Williams College noted,

> As children, teachers, and parents sprint, slink, or stumble into the new school year, they also find themselves laboring once again in the shadow of standardized tests. That is a real shame, given that there are few indications that the multiple-choice format of a typical test, in which students are quizzed on the specific formulas and bits of information they have memorized that year, actually measures what we need to know about children's education.... Instead, we should come up with assessments that truly measure the qualities of well-educated children: the ability to understand what they read; an interest in using books to gain knowledge; the capacity to know when a problem calls for mathematics and quantification; the agility to move from concrete examples to abstract principles and back again; the ability to think about a situation in several different ways; and a dynamic working knowledge of the society in which they live.

Hello Dr. Engel. Teachers have been using these types of assessments for years. They don't have to be come up with them; they already exist. From the same article:

> There is also scant evidence that these [standardized] tests encourage teachers to become better at helping individual children; in fact, some studies show that the tests protect bad teachers by hiding their lack of skill behind narrow goals and rigid scripts.

TESTING ISN'T WORKING SMARTER

In my job as a field specialist for the Fordham University Graduate School of Education, I saw what passes for education in many schools in the Bronx, under the direction and control of the forces of "corporate Taylor's scientific management," which is geared to test scores. Look at the fiasco that occurred in the New York City schools in 2010 when the New York State Board of Regents decided to apply new, tougher standards in assessing English and math "proficiency."

According to Jennifer Medina (*The New York Times*, July 28, 2010),

> More than half of public school students in New York City failed their English exams this year, and 54 percent of them passed in math. The results were in stark contrast to successes that Mayor Michael R. Bloomberg had heralded in recent years. When he ran for reelection in 2009, he boasted of state test scores that showed two-thirds of city students were passing English and 82 percent were passing math.

What are we to make of this? According to Medina,

> The scoring adjustment could raise questions about the precision of educational testing, even as policy makers across the country, including President Obama, are

relying on tests to determine teachers' pay and whether a school should be shut. In New York City, scores on state tests have been used to assign grades A through F to each school, as well as to determine principal and teacher bonuses. And the results could cast doubts on the city's improvements over the past several years; both the mayor and the schools chancellor, Joel I. Klein, have used increases in state test scores as evidence that schools have improved.

Bloomberg responded at his press conference, 'This doesn't mean the kids did any worse — quite the contrary, what this is simply saying is that we've redefined what our objectives are for the kids.' 'Whether the new expectations will instigate all of us to try harder,' he added, 'one can only hope.'

What does that mean? Have our educational leaders really redefined their objectives? Were they simply setting the bar too low to boost their political standing? Is the New York State bar set high enough? Are teachers and students going to have to work harder? Or, perhaps it is time for a new, old approach...to work smarter. Will educational leaders continue to create a two-tiered education system, or will they finally understand what it takes to educate our kids for the twenty-first century?

So what kind of assessment is authentic?

Grant Wiggins's authentic assessment is fundamentally based on what Thomas Gilbert wrote in his 1978 book, *Human Competence*. Wiggins believes that all assessments (not only tests) are best used as a means of giving feedback, which is absolutely necessary for successful learning.

According to Wiggins:

Assessment is authentic when we directly examine student performance on worthy intellectual tasks.

Do we want to evaluate student problem-posing and problem-solving in mathematics? Experimental research in science? Speaking, listening, and facilitating a discussion? Doing document-based historical inquiry? Thoroughly revising a piece of imaginative writing until it 'works' for the reader? Then let our assessment be built out of such exemplary intellectual challenges.

The best tests always teach students and teachers alike the kind of work that most matters; they are enabling and forward-looking, not just reflective of prior teaching.

> Authentic tasks involve 'ill-structured' challenges and roles that help students rehearse for the complex ambiguities of the 'game' of adult and professional life.

> Authentic assessments present the student with the full array of tasks that mirror the priorities and challenges found in the best instructional activities: conducting research; writing, revising and discussing papers; providing an engaging oral analysis of a recent political event; collaborating with others on a debate, etc.

> Further comparisons with traditional standardized tests will help to clarify what 'authenticity' means when considering assessment design and use:

> Authentic assessments attend to whether the student can craft polished, thorough and justifiable answers, performances, or products. Conventional tests typically only ask the student to select or write correct responses--irrespective of reasons.

> Authentic assessment achieves validity and reliability by emphasizing and standardizing the appropriate criteria for scoring such (varied) products; traditional testing standardizes objective 'items' and, hence, the (one) right answer for each.

> 'Test validity' should depend in part upon whether the test simulates real-world 'tests' of ability. Validity on most multiple-choice tests is determined merely by matching items to the curriculum content (or through

sophisticated correlations with other test results). (Grant Wiggins,1990, 2[2])

Wiggins was the next big thing in the 1990s and early 2000s, until the "new reformers" took hold. Actually, Wiggins had only codified what many master teachers and teacher trainers knew for a long time. Assessments (tests) had a sole purpose: to improve student achievement. The data driven by assessments must lead to feedback given to the student for them to improve.

As he says, "Authentic assessment is based upon the premise that assessment should primarily support the needs of learners. Thus, secretive tests composed of proxy items and scores that have no obvious meaning or usefulness undermine teachers' ability to improve instruction and students' ability to improve their performance. We rehearse for and teach to authentic tests--think of music, [sports], and military training--without compromising validity" (ibid.). It is the purpose and design of standardized tests that Wiggins and most master educators are concerned about. Wiggins points out, "Authentic assessments require students to be effective performers with acquired knowledge. Traditional tests tend to reveal only whether the student can recognize, recall or 'plug in' what was learned out of context. This may be as problematic as inferring driving or teaching ability from written tests alone. (Note, therefore, that the debate is not "either-or": there may well be virtue in an array of local and state assessment instruments as befits the purpose of the measurement)" (ibid.).

Engle (remember Engle?) further states,

> In recent years, psychologists have found ways to measure things as subtle as the forces that govern our moral choices and the thought processes that underlie unconscious stereotyping....For instance, using recordings of children's everyday speech, developmental psychologists can calculate two important indicators of intellectual functioning: the grammatical complexity of their sentences, and the size of their working vocabularies (not the words they circle during a test, but the ones they use

in their real lives). Why not do the same in schools? We could even employ a written version, analyzing random samples of children's essays and stories. (Engel, *The New York Times*, 2010)

Teachers already do these. They listen to and engage students in participatory class exchanges and written essays. It is bizarre to me that even with her positive spirit, this procedure is suggested as if it is a new idea, when it has been done so often by so many.

Engel then goes on to say,

Of course, these new assessments could include some paper-and-pencil work as well. But that work would have to measure students' thinking skills, not whether they can select a right answer from preset options. For instance, children could write essays in response to a prompt like, 'Choose something you are good at, and describe to your reader how you do it.' That would allow each student to draw on his area of expertise, show his ability to analyze the process, describe a task logically, and convey real information and substance. In turn, a prompt of, 'Write a description of yourself from your mother's point of view,' would help gauge the child's ability to understand the perspectives of others. (Engel, www.nytimes.com/2010/09/20/opinion /20engel.html

Again, these techniques are not new; teachers have been using them for quite some time. Why is it that they have not been given credit for these types of assessments, even in this anti-standardized test argument?

The Tasmanian Department of Education (Australia) is an example of how other nations are way ahead in thinking about what reform really is. Many of the best school districts in the United States also used these same principles. His points are best understood through his theory of "Understanding by Design." It is a concept powerful enough to be published by the Association for Supervision and Curriculum Development (ASCD) (http://www.grantwiggins.org/ubd/ubd.lasso).

"Understanding by Design" (UbD) is a framework for improving student achievement. Emphasizing the teacher's critical role as a designer of student learning, UbD works within the standards-driven curriculum to help teachers clarify learning goals, devise revealing assessments of student understanding, and craft effective and engaging learning activities.

Wiggins's "Understanding by Design" is also his codification of many of the teaching techniques already described in earlier chapters. In fact, virtually every social studies teacher trained in New York City schools since the mid-1940s was doing just that. It's how I was trained when I started in 1970. We called it the developmental lesson. What did we know? We just taught the way we were trained. (Too bad I didn't write then, I could have been a rich man.)

What follows are excerpts from a Tasmanian Department of Education guide in how to implement Wiggins's Backward Design. The parallels to good teaching as earlier described should be very clear. They used *Understanding by Design* by Grant Wiggins and Jay McTighe, which was published in 2005 by Pearson Education and the Association for Supervision and Curriculum Development. These ideas are not new. Great master teachers in many US schools have followed them for many years. Don't believe the propaganda the data-driven reformers are handing out. Their goals are more political than educational. To get students of all ability levels to succeed, this is all we really have to do: "One starts with the end -- the desired results (goals or standards) -- and then derives the curriculum from the evidence of learning (performances) called for by the standard and the teaching needed to equip students to perform (Wiggins and McTighe 2000, 8). They go on to elucidate:

The design process involves teachers planning in 3 stages, each with a focusing question:

Stage 1--What is worthy and requiring of understanding?
Stage 2--What is evidence of understanding?
Stage 3--What learning experiences and teaching promote understanding, interest, and excellence?

Enduring understandings:

1. Represent a big idea having enduring value beyond the classroom
2. Reside at the heart of the discipline (involve 'doing' the subject)
3. Require 'uncoverage' (of abstract or often misunderstood ideas)
4. Offer potential for engaging students

Students truly understand when they:

1. Can explain
2. Can interpret
3. Can apply
4. Have perspective
5. Can empathize
6. Have self-knowledge (ibid.)

This part of the planning process is what makes backward design quite different from conventional planning processes. Before planning learning experiences to develop understandings, teachers are required to plan a range of assessments. While the emphasis is clearly on developing performance tasks, Wiggins and McTighe advocate a balanced use of assessment, including more traditional forms, such as observation, quizzes, tests, etc. The range of assessment tasks and performances selected must support students in developing understanding and give students opportunities to demonstrate that understanding. The tasks must also identify and differentiate levels or degrees of understanding. An important emphasis is that assessment is part of the learning process and should occur throughout the sequence, not just at the end.

In the third stage of the backward design process, teachers design the sequence of learning experiences that students will undertake to develop understanding. The learning experiences require the students to: "[T]heorize, interpret, use, or see in perspective what they are asked to learn... (or) they will not likely understand it or grasp that their job is more than recall" (Wiggins and McTighe 2000, 100).

Experiences must blend depth and breadth, and may require choices and compromises. Those experiences that are undertaken for depth might require students to unearth, analyze, question, prove, and generalize. Those giving breadth require students to make connections, to picture (represent or model) and to extend (go beyond). Ask yourself, what are today's reformers, with teach-for-the-test principles (principals?) as a guide, doing for our children? To what extent do the assessments provide fair, valid, reliable, and sufficient measures of the desired results? Consider:

- Are students asked to exhibit their understanding through authentic performance tasks?

- Are appropriate, criterion-based, scoring tools used to evaluate student products and performances?

- Are various, appropriate, assessment formats used to provide additional evidence of learning?

- Are the assessments used as feedback for students and teachers, as well as for evaluation?

- Are students encouraged to self-assess?

The emphasis of these techniques is clearly on an inquiry-based approach that requires "uncovering" the chosen content. Assessments are both a tool to quantify student success, and more importantly, are a tool to develop student understanding through feedback and reinforcement (http://www. ltag.education.tas.gov.au/planning/models/princbackdesign.htm.).

Putting your students in a position to succeed by teaching to the test doesn't usually work. There is a big difference between teaching and testing (using a variety of methods) and teaching to tests. At the core of this difference is understanding, not rote memorization. Brain studies show that teaching and more immediate testing improves long-term memory. They also show that lessons, practice activities, and tests that mix ideas and skills lead to improved memory, and obviously better test results.

> Varying the type of material studied in a single sitting — alternating, for example, among vocabulary, reading, and speaking in a new language — seems to leave a deeper impression on the brain than does concentrating on just

one skill at a time. Musicians have known this for years, and their practice sessions often include a mix of scales, musical pieces, and rhythmic work. Many athletes, too, routinely mix their workouts with strength, speed and skill drills. . . .

...In a study recently posted online by the journal *Applied Cognitive Psychology*, Doug Rohrer and Kelli Taylor of the University of South Florida taught a group of fourth-graders four equations, each to calculate a different dimension of a prism. Half of the children learned by studying repeated examples of one equation, say, calculating the number of prism faces when given the number of sides at the base, then moving on to the next type of calculation, studying repeated examples of that. The other half studied mixed problem sets, which included examples of all four types of calculations grouped together. Both groups solved sample problems along the way, as they studied. A day later, the researchers gave all of the students a test on the material, presenting new problems of the same type. The children who had studied mixed sets did twice as well as the others, out-scoring them 77 percent to 38 percent. The researchers have found the same in experiments involving adults and younger children. 'When students see a list of problems, all of the same kind, they know the strategy to use before they even read the problem,' said Dr. Rohrer. 'That's like riding a bike with training wheels.' With mixed practice, he added, 'each problem is different from the last one, which means kids must learn how to choose the appropriate procedure — just like they had to do on the test.'

These findings extend well beyond math, even to aesthetic intuitive learning. In an experiment published last month in the journal *Psychology and Aging*, researchers found that college students and adults of retirement age were better able to distinguish the painting styles of twelve unfamiliar artists after viewing mixed collections (assortments, including works from all twelve) than after viewing a dozen works from one artist, all together, then moving on to the next painter. When a student understands the content and process used to work with that particular content, they can handle any question in any format. They can solve and discuss any problem or issue or concept. (B. Carey, "Forget What You Know About Good Study Habits," *The New York Times,* September 6, 2010)

Again, Engle makes a strong point,

By shifting our assessment techniques, we would learn more of what we really need to know about how children, teachers, and schools are doing. And testing could be returned to its rightful place as one tool among many for improving schools, rather than serving as a weapon that degrades the experience for teachers and students alike. (Engel 2010)

Thus, backward planning with built-in assessments that test a variety of skills and ideas will lead to increased student achievement. Try it. Not only will you like it, but so will your students. They will learn more, understand more, and be more successful. As a result, they will enjoy learning more and feel better about themselves as students. That is real self-esteem. And, by the way, they, without stressful test training, will do far better on those tests.

I AM THE SEED SHE PLANTED

William Wordsworth wrote in his famous poem, *The Rainbow,* "The child is the father of the man." We could just as easily say, "The student is the father of the teacher." Just as human traits are established while young, so are teacher traits.

All I ever needed to learn about who I am as a human and as a teacher, I learned, not in kindergarten, but in second grade. Truth be told, I don't remember much of kindergarten and first grade, except nap time, blocks, being scolded for not wanting to nap, and having my first-grade teacher tell my mother that I needed "testing." I was never sure what my first-grade teacher, Mrs. S. (the bunned witch), meant by that. I think she meant psychological. It was before attention deficit disorder (ADD) was the easy answer. I prefer to think that she meant gifted and talented. Turns out it was probably a bit of both.

It was there that I endured Mrs. S. in class 1-3. I have one class picture of me in a cowboy outfit. I was smiling. It must have been Halloween. Like I said, I don't remember much of first grade. I do remember not liking her and school. My memories consist of being told to keep my hands folded on the desk and my legs under it. That was hard, because the desks were bolted to the floor, and I didn't fit. So, I kept moving my feet and legs into the aisle, for which I was scolded time and time again. "David. Put your feet under your desk. You will trip someone." I would usually respond, "But no one is allowed to get up and walk down the aisle." At which point, she would tell me to be quiet and, "behave yourself." So, I would be quiet and not pay much attention, rather than get yelled at, until the next time I had to move my oversized legs from under the undersized desk.

Actually, I don't remember much of third, fourth, or sixth grades either. I skipped fifth grade. I guess I really was gifted. I only remember sixth grade because of two reasons. One was a guy named Murray, who did the dumbest things. He was hysterical. In fact, we created a new phrase, to "pull a Murray," which meant doing something Murray-like. (Thirteen years later, I nicknamed my wife Murray.) The second and most important reason turned out to be my most embarrassing moment in school. You know, the one when you want to hide, not only under the screwed-to-the-floor-desks, but under the floor they were screwed into. Mrs. F. was going over some spelling list I was not particularly interested in. Actually, after second grade, there wasn't much in school I was interested in, except playing ball in the school yard. My second-grade teacher spoiled me.

Anyway, Mrs. F. was giving each person in the room a word to spell and pronounce. "Oh no," I thought. There were enough words to reach me in my seat in the last row; I figured out which word I was going to have to spell and pronounce. "Oh shit," I thought. "I have no idea how to pronounce it: *a.w.k.w.a.r.d.* What kind of 'fuckin' word is that?" I had never seen it, heard it spoken, let alone knew its meaning. Pretty ironic, huh? "Hmm, is it *owkword? Awwwkwaaard?*" (As you can tell, I learned to curse early on in life. That was far more useful than knowing *awwwkwerd.*)

"Oh no. Does she see how panicked I am? I don't have a clue," and now she says, "David, please do word number twenty-six," or whatever number it was. I fumbled for the right pronunciation, screwed it up, spelled it, then, as we all had to do back then, say it again... incorrectly, while listening to the belly laughs of my classmates and Mrs. Bitch telling me to try again. And again. And again. Remember when I said I had skipped fifth grade? Well, that made it even worse. Not only was I the youngest in my class by about one and a half years, but I was also in a class with very few cronies who knew how smart I really was. As a result, I never forgot this experience. It was a moment that probably led me to teaching, although I didn't realize it back then.

That takes me back to second grade. Miss Stafford was our teacher. She must have been the ripe, old age of twenty-three. We had no idea. We were seven. In 1956 and 1957, she was ancient. She was also incredible. When she passed away in 2009, several of us from her second-grade class were at her memorial service. We had no idea that our Miss Stafford would become the world renown Dr. Rita Dunn. A professor at St. John's University for nearly forty years, she had become an authority on learning styles, an internationally renowned professor of higher education, a prolific author of thirty-two textbooks and more than four hundred fifty manuscripts and research papers, and the recipient of thirty-one professional research awards. We had no idea who she was going to become. At the time, neither did she. I wrote this in her Tribute Book:

> Little did we know as seven-year-olds entering Rita Stafford's class 2-1 in PS 66, Bronx, in September of 1956, that we were to become the happy guinea pigs for a life dedicated to helping children with all kinds of 'personalities,' as we called it then.

People marvel when they are told of what Rita did for us. They marvel at our advanced work. They marvel at our activities. They marvel at our reunions every Christmas time for twelve years, and at our last reunion, eight years ago this month. [Forty-four years after our second-grade class.]

I can't count the number of times I have told students and teaching colleagues how we learned about the solar system by building one and hanging it from the ceiling; or about civil rights by writing letters to President Eisenhower. (We even received a reply and were quoted in *The New York Times*.)

She inspired me to become a teacher. Those activities were the seeds of every 'outrageous' activity I ever cooked up for use in my classrooms. The more I look back on my body of teaching and work, the more I see how indebted I am to her. I used a variety of styles because I knew, not intrinsically, but because I experienced it in her second-grade classroom, that they were necessary to reach more kids.

Over the past dozen years or so, I have become increasingly interested in the rise of the number of under-achieving boys in our society. The more I read about the subject, the more I realize that she was right on the money those fifty-three years ago. Both directly as a teacher, and indirectly, through her research and training sessions, she saved countless students from failure. I know she saved me.

Over the years, I have never stopped talking about her. In addition to students and teachers, I have spoken about her to several colleagues involved in this latest endeavor. I have told the Teach For America teachers I mentor in the Bronx about her. She is their model.

I will continue to tell everyone I know about her. She was my hero. My work shall forever be in her honor and name.

She proved to me that in any one year, any one teacher could make a difference to any one student. She was creative and autonomous. She was innovative and caring. Unfortunately, I didn't have many other teachers who had a positive impact on my life. Most were and still are forgotten. Looking back I now understand how being a student totally influenced who I became as a teacher.

There weren't many I learned from or remember having any influence on me besides "Miss Stafford. One, most cool, was Mr. Gerard, the Junior High music teacher who could play two reed instruments at the same time in two-part harmony. He was a character. He used to take us into the huge clothing closet if we were "acting up" and whisper, "shh, just make noises like I am hurting you." Then he would throw stuff and bang on the walls. Although it was an act we got hip to rather fast, it made him rate high on the cool-but-nuts factor. Another lesson learned--always make them think you are crazier than they are.

I went to the Bronx High School of Science. I hated it. I did poorly-- for there. Out of a class of 950, I ranked 903rd, with an average of about 80 percent. Even if I had an 85 average, a solid B, I would have been in the bottom half of the class. I spent more time playing basketball, softball, and touch football at the schoolyards with my Black and Puerto Rican neighborhood buddies. When I was in school, I was mostly bored. I was also immature and hadn't yet learned how to "do school." I had always gotten by on innate ability. I had no idea how to study, write, do home-work correctly, or even really engage in class work. I was virtually left to my own devices. The fact that I was influenced how I taught.

Only four teachers interested me and improved my learning. Mr. Merovick was the social studies chairperson and a master teacher. His discussion-based American history class was all about how we developed points of view. Mr. Kotkin turned microbiology into fun-filled "piss and puncture." Those two influenced me.

Mr. Rifkin, an English teacher, made studying Othello intriguing. To this day, it is the only play of Shakespeare I enjoyed reading, because of him. One day, he asked us why we thought we were studying Othello. I whispered, "to kill time," to the student seated to my immediate left. Mr. Rifkin heard it, and for another year, every time he saw me in the hall, he would ask, in a good-natured way, "Hey Greene, still killing time?" From him, I learned the power of great hearing and a sense of self-deprecating humor. Finally, there was Mrs. Rockow, the only teacher I asked to sign my yearbook. She was my senior-year math teacher who showed me how to use my abilities to tackle sold geometry and probability. No one had tapped my brain that way before. It was her way of differentiation, and I learned how that personal touch is so important in turning students around.

Sometimes, just as we parent as a reaction to what we hated about how our parents treated us, teachers learn to do the same. Certainly I didn't want to follow in the footsteps of my first and sixth grade teachers. I also learn what not to do from another bunned teacher, who embarrassed me what seemed daily in class. Mr. C., my economics teacher, was infamous for setting the world record for "*Ums*" in a forty-minute period--436. He, by the way, has one distinguishing, positive accomplishment. He was the second teacher who pointed me to my career path. I remember saying one day that I could do a better job than he. I didn't make much of that back then, but as things turned out, it became true.

Just as our experiences as a child influence how we parent, our experiences as a young student influence how we teach. The problem as I see it is that too many new teachers take on the bad habits of too many teachers they had as students.

I KNOW GREAT TEACHING WHEN I SEE IT

Who remembers their favorite test from school? You know, the one that inspired you to become who you are now, or saved you from the wrong part of yourself? Who remembers the test that made you want to come out of your shell? Which test gave you the courage to try new things and challenge yourself? For me, it was the *1966 Regents Comprehensive Examination in Social Studies*.

Ok, only kidding. We all know that it is teachers who inspire and challenge us to be our best. It isn't testing, or much of what is now being called teaching. We also know which teachers did that. We might remember some incidents in their classes, or things they said or wrote to us. Do we remember the everyday things? The attitude they brought to the room? Their techniques?

When I see former students (from the Bronx to Scarsdale), they don't tell me about the Goals or Aim or Motivation from October 23rd, 2002. They will tell me about my energy, my excitement, my caring, and my prodding them to do their best, not to settle for mediocrity. They tell me about a particular project that inspired or challenged them to think critically, or do things they never thought they could. They even remember what they learned while doing those things. What they don't know is how all of that was planned.

Doug Lemov is right. "Great teaching is an art." But he is wrong when he tries to turn this art into a science of 49 great techniques (Doug Lemov's *Teach Like a Champion, 49 Techniques that Put Students on the Path to College*, 2010). Of course, there are great techniques that have been used by great teachers, but it isn't the technique that makes the teacher great. It is what the great teacher brings to the technique. I have watched these techniques used perfectly in perfectly horrible lessons and marginally well in absolutely magnificent lessons, because of who the teacher is as much as what the teacher does. This is true, whatever the teacher's age or experience level. Teaching is as much talent as it is skill.

Let's look at Mr. Lemov's (2010, 9-10) comment fearing teachers being "distracted by the qualities of the activity.... Great teachers plan objectives, then assessments, then activities." That is true. What is also important is the quality of the activities and your probing, challenging, written, and oral questions. It is all one big package. How does that lesson or activity, as simple or complex as it may be, get your kids to learn and understand those objectives and succeed on the assessments?

So, what is a good teacher? The sum of all those things. Each and every day a good teacher is a motivator, planner, questioner, assessor, mother or father, even entertainer. Plan accordingly. It is the key. Your kids rely on that. But don't make it look too planned.

Lemov asks, "Who would look at a chisel, a mallet, and a file, and imagine them producing Michelangelo's David?" Put them in Michelangelo's hands, and you have a work of art. Put those tools in my hands, and you get crushed rock. So many so-called educational reformers believe that given their version of the right tools, techniques, and tests, any top college student can become a successful teacher.

I learned from several esteemed mentors that the best teachers never stopped learning and listening. How else can we find out what makes good teaching, but by listening to people from both sides of the desk? In researching this book, I reached out to many people and asked these simple questions:

As a student:

1. What made your best teachers your best teachers? Consider personal characteristics, techniques, activities, and relationships with students. What made your worst teachers your worst teachers? Consider personal characteristics, techniques, activities, and relationships with students.

2. From which teachers did you learn the most? Why? From which teachers did you learn the least? Why? (You don't have to name names.)

3. Please describe any particularly positive or negative classroom moments or activities that stand out. What made them so memorable?

I received a wide variety of answers from friends, family, colleagues, and former students. I wasn't quite sure what to expect, but I have been saying for years to anyone who will listen that all you have to do to improve education is to ask people what made their best teachers best, then train teachers to do as many of those replicable things as possible. Two things cannot be replicated, though: personality and natural talent. Although personality and natural talent cannot be learned, teachers certainly can be taught to use what works best for them as individuals.

Hard as it was, I selected what I thought were the clearest messages and tried to list them by six essential categories: Challenge, Engagement,

Interaction, Personality, Personal Touch, and Planning. These are listed in alphabetical order, because they are equally important.

Challenge:

- The best teachers build a relationship with their students by challenging them.

- The best teacher puts you in a position to succeed.

- They actually cared about my success and did not allow for the possibility of failure by setting high expectations. This made a lifelong impact on my life.

- The best teachers paced the class at a level that worked for everyone. In hindsight, it seems magical, apparent more when absent. I'm aware of teachers who kept everyone challenged, but more aware of teachers where I felt like the material was moving too slowly or too quickly for me to handle. In the latter case, the result (on my part) was boredom or frustration--and in both cases, a loss of interest in the topic. But in the former case, the result was challenge, pride in my work, and a feeling of accomplishment.

- The best teachers are those that lead the student to water but force them to get to the end on their own.

- The ones that I learned the most were the ones who challenged me, who wouldn't let me just take the easy route, who were patient yet firm, who didn't cosign my BS and let me get away with mediocrity.

Engagement:

- The best teachers came in prepared and eager to reach out. You felt that they loved what they were doing. I learned most from the ones who were able to engage the classroom.

- Kids know if you want to be there.

- The best classroom is one where students can think, question, and make those personal and meaningful connections.

- They used clear, vivid language--some of their phrases I remember over forty years later. They loved engaging in debate with their students.

- My best teachers were always engaging, relying on interactive teaching methods to best gain the interest of the students.

- One significant quality that I admire was that they saw teaching as an adventure, constantly questioning, having fun doing it, and that it had real- life relevance.

- My best teachers were the teachers who were open and willing to reach their students on the student level. They were the teachers who best understood how we, as students, were still growing and learning--and making mistakes. They were the teachers who made an effort to appreciate us as individuals and recognize us for our own talents and interests.

Interaction:

- A great lesson is one in which there is student participation and connection between student and teacher.

- They use active interaction with students.

- They did not "lecture" at us--but spoke with us--used real-life examples, allowed us to speak freely, even if we disagreed. They fostered participation and real discourse.

- A lesson is great when there is enough opportunity for authentic interaction between students, teachers, and other students.

- Interactive teaching where students can chime in with their questions and thoughts, while maintaining a sense of direction and achieving teaching goals.

- I learned a lot from teachers who let us into their world and their interests--it made them more relatable. I learned the least from the teachers I did not have more than a classroom relationship with. I now realize that the most significant learning experiences I had in high school were with the teachers that I connected with.

Personality:

- The best teachers were any teachers who seemed authentic, who seemed to really walk the walk as well as talk the talk.

- My best teachers were teachers that gave me knowledge, not only by textbook, but also with humor. They create activities that apply knowledge.

- They have a good sense of humor. They make learning fun.

- The best teachers have a big personality. You can see that they are excited by what they do!

- I enjoyed those teachers who clearly *enjoyed* teaching, i.e., they themselves weren't bored with what they were doing, but rather projected a love for their subject--and their subjects [students].

- The personal characteristic of my best teachers was that they loved their job, and it was evident in their teaching style. They love to see the student "get it."

- It seems that the best atmospheres were those where the teacher had both a personal relationship with students and (somewhat contradictory) complete control of the classroom.

- My best teachers were enthusiastic about their subjects--they cared deeply, and made us want to care also.

- They knew how to play with and poke fun at the students, to keep the atmosphere light and easy.

- Teachers who like students are generally successful.

- Many of my best teachers possessed integrity, humor, and consistency.

The Personal Touch:

- Kids pick up on attitudes and can usually cut through the facade. When kids feel genuinely cared about by a teacher, they think the teacher is a good teacher.

- The best teacher, whether teaching science, math, or football is the one who can bring out the best in me, and take my worst, and show me how to make it better. The best teacher finds qualities in the not-so gifted student that allows that student to see that he, too, can succeed. The great teachers showed an interest in us, but did not overdo it by trying to be "our friends." The great teachers used their personal life experience to help us grow and mature.

- The best teachers gave attention, not just to the subject, but also to the real academic needs of me, as a student, as a growing person. The best allowed me to express myself creatively without judgment, and enforce critical-thinking skills. They knew how to make demands to elevate my skills, abilities, and responsibilities as a student. They were personal, without losing sight of their role as teachers, mentors, and guiders of the academic spirit. They would build and not tear down. They understood the journey a young person needed to take to get to the bridge in preparation for the next phase of development... they inspired this by their actions.

- Clearly, they were experts in their chosen field and were enthusiastic about the content, which translated many times to the students also being enthusiastic about the content.

Planning:

- They use innovative teaching methods.

- They keep the kids interested. A great lesson is one where the class is working along with the teacher.

- A great lesson plan connects planning, questioning, and activities to doing, action, and reflection.

- A lesson is great when it is well planned. One has to consider all the ways children learn. Teachers have to know their students, and provide them all opportunities.

- A great lesson is one that is well planned but is flexible enough to leave room for the "teachable" moment or for situations that would make a change of direction needed.

- I think a variety of activities are needed, both to keep the interest of the students and to find ways of reaching all different kinds of learners.

- Higher-level questions on all grade levels are important, and I never saw enough of these used by student teachers.

- Get to know your students' learning styles and what seems to hold their interest and challenge them. This valuable information will help with how to plan your lessons, and the types of questioning and activities you use. The types of learners in your class will dictate the lessons you plan. I guess you would call this customizing your lessons to your particular students.

- All types of lessons can work, but no one technique should be used always.

Finally, one note on school atmosphere:

- The best atmospheres are supportive and self-directing and that develop a sense of professionalism and camaraderie among colleagues.

That last comment is significant. Schools and districts must create those types of atmospheres to allow teachers to be their best. Am I too Pollyannaish to think that is not that hard to do? No.

Teaching is learning how to be that person. Teachers, young and old, new or experienced, can become better at what they do by listening to and observing the best teachers do those things well. If they are lucky enough to be in a supportive and self-directing school atmosphere that develops a sense of professionalism and camaraderie among colleagues, they will become among the best in their profession.

TEACHING TEACHERS TEACHING

Several TFA CMs have successfully pulled themselves to safety because they aren't followers. They are the critically thinking problem solvers good teachers must be. They have practical wisdom; they have empathy. They clearly try to use, not fight, the cultural baggage their students carry to school. They also have to be lucky enough to be in the right school with the right leadership. That necessitates more principals who really are principal teachers, not in name only. They must be people who are willing to listen to educators--not administrative, bureaucratic, pencil-pushing, bean counters. They must read, research, and understand where real staff development comes from, then go out and get it without fear of reprisal. It is a pleasure to work with young teachers in schools that foster this type of growth, which work to encourage rigorous yet relevant, inquiry, discussion, and project-based learning (PBL). But most importantly, they need help.

EXPERIENCED MENTORS

I graduated from Fordham University's undergraduate School of Education in 1970. The program no longer exists. Our four years included heavy academic work in our subject area, class work in pedagogy, and fieldwork in local neighborhood, afternoon centers. All of that was before you began a full-time, semester-long internship as a student teacher. The pedagogy classes weren't worth much, but that's true in all schools of education. I have always believed that more practical experience with great teachers beats theory taught in an ivory tower. University education programs must get with the program. The ivory tower is too blinded by its own light. They must retool and develop more in-school mentor programs rather than rely on pedagogy classes that, well, for the most part, are less than helpful. They have to put more emphasis on fieldwork and intern-ship work, and less on class work. If schools of education want to improve teaching they must make teaching training more similar to the other "life saving" professions, plumbing and medicine. They both include long periods of apprenticeships and ongoing certification before permanent licensing. As long as they think PhD academics are more important than teacher training, things won't change much.

A major difference between my generation and present-day TFA Corps Members was that I gradually entered teaching. I wasn't dumped into the quicksand up to my neck. I was extremely lucky to have a cooperating teacher, Phyllis Opochinsky, (think hospital attending physician) a young master who, in turn, had been trained by an older master, Mr. Milton Belasco, chairman of the social studies department and author of textbooks and Regents review books. Unknowingly, I became part of the chain that passed down "practical wisdom" from one teacher generation to the next.

The first few weeks, I did nothing but watch her, learn from her work, and practice writing lesson plans with her. I was then, on occasion, allowed to teach one of her classes. Then, for the last quarter, I took over one of her classes as my own, but always with her in the room: By law, she had to be there. More importantly--she was there for me. We had pre- and post class discussions to work on improving my techniques. As good as that experience was, it should have lasted a full year. There is no better way to learn to teach than by this process: having a master cooperating teacher at your side, letting you fail, helping you succeed, coaxing, pushing, and teaching you how to teach. It is how many generations of great New York City teachers were made. Somehow, this process was lost over the past couple of decades. Perhaps, it will now be regenerated.

The second difference was where and for whom I worked when I started my first job, at the brand new Adlai E. Stevenson High School, also in the South Bronx. As far as the public knew, we were the gang-filled, violence-laden school with championship basketball teams whose leading players, Ed Pinckney (currently a coach for the Chicago Bulls) and Fred Brown (now a successful financial advisor in the DC area) became famous playing for Villanova, the Boston Celtics, and Georgetown. We were stereotyped. The reality was that it was a great place to teach, to learn to teach and to go to school.

My immediate supervisor, Department Chair and Assistant Principal Bertram Linder, and my principal, Leonard Littwin, were also master teachers of social studies and gifted mentors of new teachers. Together, they gave me the foundation to become a confident teacher in my field of study. They also gave me academic freedom. They trusted my intelligence and creativity. As a result, I knew I could grow, and grow I did.

When I started in Stevenson, I was given a lousy schedule. I was to teach world history to the least academically motivated ninth-graders in the school. There were no mentors. My only assistance was to come from my department chairman, Bert Linder. As a non-tenured teacher, I could be observed informally as often as he wished. Formally, I believe, he had to do at least three a semester. Thank God he did. I survived because of him and the Vince Lombardi of principals, Leonard Littwin. Bert's visits and follow-up discussions gave me confidence by telling me he knew I would--as a first-year teacher--make lots of mistakes, but I had the essential tools to become a great teacher. He gave me responsibilities, gave me reviews to write for the *Journal of New York City Teachers of Social Studies*, and saved my ass more than once.

For example, one very hot, Friday afternoon, I had an eighth- (last) period class. They clearly didn't want to be there. One student decided to "test" me by walking up to a window, opening it, and climbing on to the sill. As I stood there dumbfounded, my department chair (Mr. Linder) walked in the room to observe me. "Oh shit," I thought; I was finished. Monday I'd be driving a cab. Bert stayed and watched the class I could barely control, let alone teach. When the class ended, he told me to see him later. Later turned out to be Monday. Surely, I was going to be given a U (unsatisfactory).

When I met with him on Monday, he said three things. First, how bad my lesson was. Second, he wasn't going to count it as an observation, because he remembered teaching classes like that when he was younger. Third, we discussed how to use my personal strengths to counteract what technical weaknesses I had because I was new. He encouraged me by saying that once my technique caught up with what I brought to the classroom, I would be the master others could come to learn from. And I thought I was to be fired.

Stevenson's principal Leonard Littwin scared people, but Lenny knew teaching. He was blunt and direct. He sat in the back of classrooms, watching and taking notes. He was a master social studies teacher before he became an administrator. His goal, which he filtered down to his department chairs, was to develop as many talented teachers as possible. Mostly, he succeeded. Many succeeded to pass on what they learned, including me. What he told me, he must have shared with hundreds of teachers over the years. He asked three essential questions:

- What do you want your students to know, understand, do, and communicate by the end of your class?

- How are you going to assess those?

- What do you want them buzzing about as they leave, so that they want more tomorrow?

With those questions as our focus, we discussed how projected outcomes, goals, and objectives are to be achieved and measured using authentic assessments (essay writing, projects of all sorts, and even multiple-choice and short-answer questions). These three fundamental questions still define great teaching, regardless of what the new "data driven" reform movement says.

How ironic that, in the fall of 2008, I found myself mentoring a TFA Corps Member in the "campus" that once was A.E. Stevenson. Many of the old offices were converted into classrooms. My mentee and I were sitting in his classroom, which at one time was Littwin's old office. Lo and behold, what comes out of my mouth? "What do you want your students to know, understand, do, and communicate by the end of your class?" "How are you going to assess those?" "What do you want them buzzing about as they leave, so that they want more tomorrow?" Our subsequent discussions about what was necessary to make those happen was the basis for my mentee's success in that school and subsequent hiring in a school of his choice. Over the past forty-two years, I have worked with several student teachers and nineteen TFA Corps Members. Their success is not due to anything more than my passing forward what I have learned from those old masters from Stevenson.

These teacher-leader principals cannot do it alone. Schools need a real mentoring program. In theory, New York City schools have one. In practice, it often doesn't exist. As an example, one TFA Corps Member who taught middle school social studies had a physical education teacher as a mentor because "he comes in to quiet them down." Who are these mentors going to be, when schools don't have enough high quality, experienced teachers to go around?

There are thousands of retired, high-quality teachers willing to do become mentors. Why not use the expertise of retired, potential F-Status teachers? According to the New York City Department of Education, F-Status is defined as: *"A per diem employee engaged for a full term but for less than five full days per week"*. The reality is that most F-Status people substitute, do paper work, and are often cronies not well chosen for the little "mentoring" they may do. We are told that would be too expensive. More often than not, the money is paid instead to for-profit, cookie-cutter, lesson-plan providers.

Now, I fear that is all disappearing. Will there be any "old" masters left to pass forward what makes great teaching? Will there be any Littwins, Linders, or even Greenes left to pass on what they learned from those before them? Will there be any lifetime teachers? Will public education as we knew it be crushed and replaced by a system of short-term, temporary, robotic teachers who simply follow a conveyor-belt script in this new, factory like, privatized, education-for-profit system, and then move on to another job when they burn out?

Teaching is an art, to be cherished, not lost and mummified. Our students should not become guinea pigs in a *Fahrenheit 451* world of mathematical schema and "data-driven" engineering. Lifelong teachers must be allowed to continue to use our God-given abilities to think, reason, and create. Will we be allowed to, or will we, like other endangered species, just become extinct?

WORKING WITH PEERS

Another method is peer mentoring. Recently, I was an observer in a Lesson Study Group. In it a team of math student teachers collegially prepared a math lesson one of my TFA mentees (S.) was to teach. We had a pre-observation meeting, observed the class, and had a post class meeting to provide feedback. Immediately following that, the group revised the lesson, and S. went back to teach the new and improved version.

This kind of group-think may not be right for everyone. I, myself, offered the caveat that "a camel is a horse created by committee." I pointed out that the lesson needed to be less complex, and that it's imperative to throw out the less "good" ideas in a group plan, because the goal has to remain what the kids can successfully accomplish, not what would be "cool" to try. They were novices. That same method used by a team of more experienced teachers with my novice would have been far more successful.

Over the years, I have been part of another peer mentoring model called Critical Friends that follows much of the same protocol, but with the teacher as sole planner. Either way, these sessions, along with at least a semester's worth of observations of other teachers (plural), and supervised practice in an internship setting similar towhere the prospective teacher will end up, are the only ways one can learn enough about how to teach before being given one's own room. In fact, one must be judged there first, before being allowed to be licensed and able to find a job.

Teachers should be supervised, trained, and given opportunities to grow in their profession through various types of programs, not just those chosen for them by their one-track-minded supervisors. They need the opportunity to explore new ideas, go to conventions, examine multiple resources, and work with master teacher trainers from different backgrounds. That is how all professionals improve their skills. Ask doctors, psychologists, or lawyers the importance of keeping current with new techniques and ideas. Teachers should then be encouraged to try out their newly acquired skills, techniques, and ideas to continue their improvement in the classroom, and to share them with colleagues.

WISE UP.

What did you do your senior year of high school? Many of you applied to colleges, more early these days, waited for acceptances, finished whatever courses you needed to graduate, and caught the disease, Senioritis (Senior Slump). Others finished out their course work on the way to work or the military and yet still caught the disease. Others never made it to the second semester of senior year, or made it but didn't graduate because to them school was a prison from which they sought escape or a place for failure not success.

We are presently being bombarded with a call to reform education, for new and fresh ideas, for more student involvement for increased motivation, and for innovation. I am about to tell you that the most innovative, creative, and fresh answer to those questions for high school seniors is 40 years old this year. WISE ("Woodlands Individualized Senior Experience") was founded in 1972 at Woodlands High School in Greenburgh, New York by a group of students, teachers, parents and community members in order to address "senior slump" and to aid the transition of graduating seniors to life after high school.

What if, instead of sitting in or cutting those senior classes you were able to follow your passion to;

- Intern with a legendary New York Times Columnist as Andrew Ross Sorkin did

- Become a firefighter as Gina Hudson did

- Explore the physics and economics of skateboarding as Jikirta Muhammadu did

- Practice meteorology for a local meterology and aviation company as Ralph Vasami did

- Study the roots of black English at a graduate school level as Vinnie Bagwell did

These are but five of approximately 35,000 stories. Students have done WISE ("Wise Individualized Senior Experience") projects all over the United States and abroad in every subject you can imagine. What would you have chosen to do if you could do anything (affordable, legal and insurable) for academic credit?

There are now over 60 high schools in the USA that presently have WISE programs. There are almost 200 that have senior programs created based on WISE. My guess is that there are many more high schools with similar experiential learning programs. For 40 years, WISE seniors of all ability levels have created individualized real-world experiences (WISE projects), exploring their passions outside the traditional classroom. Over 35,000 WISE graduates have learned to collaborate and to work independently, developing organizational, research, writing, and presentation skills as they ignite a lifetime of personal growth.

What is WISE? WISE serves as a bridge for seniors from high school to college, work and lifelong learning. A WISE program enables high school seniors of all ability levels to design an individualized, passion-driven project. Projects can include, but are not limited to, internships, independent research, self-improvement, community service or cultural, artistic and performance-based activities. The topics students can explore in school-based, experiential learning programs are limitless. As a result, students discover in themselves and in one another skills, strengths and talents they had not realized were present. All students receive academic credit upon successful completion of their WISE project.

As part of the process of developing and completing their WISE projects, students select a staff mentor, maintain a reflective and research-supported journal and make a public presentation. During the school day, as well as in the evenings and on weekends, students devote significant time to work on their projects—they research their topics, maintain written and multimedia daily journals, meet with their mentors to explore and reflect upon project issues, and discuss their topics with one another. Upon completion of the project, each student gives a public presentation assessed by a panel of students, teachers and community members, all of whom have read the journal. Student projects provide parents and community members with real engagement in the life of the school; they offer teacher-mentors a chance to see their students apply academic skills in a real-world setting.

All WISE programs are designed, run and supported by a collaborative task force of teachers, students, administrators, parents and community members (and, in schools with long-standing programs, WISE graduates). Staff, students and community coordinators manage the day-to-day activities of their WISE program.

Any takers? By the way, Andrew Ross Sorkin is now the editor-at-large of DealBook, which he started in 2001. Mr. Sorkin is The New York Times's chief mergers and acquisitions reporter, a columnist and co-anchor of CNBC's Squawk Box. In addition, Mr. Sorkin is an assistant editor of business and finance news, helping guide and shape the paper's coverage. He is also the author of *"Too Big To Fail."* Gina Hudson is a firefighter. Ralph Vasami owns that company. Vinnie Bagwell is now an award winning sculptor whose work is on the campus of Hofstra University, prominently displayed in the cities of Memphis and Yonkers, and on the Broadway stage in August Wilson's Piano Lesson.

WISE is the single best education reform I have seen or been a part of. I saw seniors of all ability levels achieve things impossible to achieve in a regular classroom. While I taught at Woodlands two of my students did a study of the Greenburgh School District and presented it to the Board of Education. Another studied dolphins in the Florida Keys. A third explored what would happen if he, a white kid, tried to mix hard rock with hip-hop. A fourth (another white kid) worked for a new label and new record producer, Def. Jam and Russell Simmons. He became their college rep when he graduated high school. Since1973 hundreds of Woodlands seniors took advantage of this incredible and unique program

In 1991, When Vic Leviatin and Andrew Courtney (two of the WISE founders) retired, they formed WISE Services "excited by the thousands of projects [they] saw. Knowing that other schools would be interested in beginning their own programs, they started WISE Services. The first WISE Services conference for interested schools was held in May 1992, and WISE Services helped Scarsdale, Croton-Harmon and Mamaroneck design and implement senior project programs for their high schools in the spring of 1993. Over twenty years over 35,000 seniors have completed WISE projects."

While I was teaching at Woodlands teachers from Scarsdale High School came to investigate our program because they had a committee set up to investigate ways to improve their seniors' senior year experience. Then in Scarsdale, like other high schools across the nation, Senior Slump had generated and morphed into a huge problem especially since so many were college bound and knew by April, and increasingly earlier as a result of the institution of early admission.

Little did I know that a year later, when I arrived at Scarsdale, the head of that committee to help plan Scarsdale's version would approach me to be a part of that committee and help it make its recommendations to the staff, students, and administration. The task force looked at WISE and a similar program at New Trier HS (an equally affluent suburban high school outside of Chicago) at the same time Vic Leviatin and Andy Courtney had just retired from Woodlands and created WISE Services. Finally, in 1992-3 Scarsdale High School started its Senior Options program. Of course Scarsdale had to name it something other than WISE at Scarsdale or SISE (Scarsdale Individualized Senior Experience). It's a Scarsdale thing.

That program is now in its 20th year. Over the years approximately 5,500 students have done Scarsdale's version of a WISE project, including my two children. In 1999, I became the coordinator of the program until I retired. It has been one of the reasons people consider Scarsdale a great school. It is something kids come to the High School as 9th graders looking forward to doing. I challenge anyone to judge the results.

I helped WISE come to Scarsdale High School. I had no idea how doing so would lead to what may have been my biggest act of "Non sibi", the motto of the Scarsdale School District. It is Latin for "not for self". It is an ideal we try to instill in kids, to be selfless, to do for others. I guess its what all my mentors had done for me and what I had been paying forward.

On August 29th, 2005 Hurricane Katrina devastated New Orleans and the Gulf Coast. That fall, several families from Scarsdale decided to organize S.O.S. for Education to help. The schools also organized to help. As a result of a member of our district's staff contacting former colleagues in the area, the Bay Saint Louis-Waveland School District was chosen as the focal point for this joint effort. S.O.S. for Education, the community group, worked on its fundraising and school supply raising efforts, the Scarsdale schools following suit. As Coordinator of the Scarsdale High School Senior Options program, I realized that the High School had the capacity to not just raise money and goods, but also send real people to the Gulf to do what became called "Katrina Relief".

I organized a weeklong trip in June 2006 that could only have been done because we had our WISE program. Seniors had no classes or finals at that time. That year 9 seniors ended their WISE-Senior Options projects a week early and together with myself and 2 other teachers traveled to New Orleans and Bay Saint Louis Waveland for the first of what has now become a tradition. We drove through the stricken streets of New Orleans and were horrified, not only at the incredible destruction, but also of the obvious differences in neighborhoods. The lower ninth ward was a ghost town, devoid of life as well as salvageable property. Silent. No birds. No insects. No classroom could ever teach those kids what they learned that day. Neither could it teach them what they heard from the people we worked with and for in.

As a result of that trip a few students and I organized the High School SOS4EDUCATION club to organize and fundraise for trips in June and the future. The club organized school fundraising activities that raised $25,000 to not only help subsidize the June 2008 trip but also to donate $14,000 directly to the schools in Bay Saint Louis-Waveland. That year, we had over 90 students volunteer and had to hold a lottery for the 24 student placements we decided on (logistics limited the number) for that year's trip. We went from 9 students in 2006, to 15 in 2007, to 24 in 2008, 2009 and 2010 with 30 seniors on the waiting list each year and $10,000 additional donations each year.

Over the past 40 years overall, WISE has been given accolades from all circles, including the NYS Education Department, the NY Times, Phi Delta Kappan, and TIME magazine. Jo Anne Larson of the NYS Education department said in her letter dated 11/5/1993,

> "The students and parents who have participated in the Individualized Senior Experiences are telling spokespersons for the program. It is rare that one finds individuals who remain enthusiastic supporters of a school program years after they themselves have been participants."

Eric Bassin, a former student at Woodlands grew up to be a teacher and has coordinated WISE programs at both Milken High School in Los Angeles and Solomon Schechter High School in NY, talked about his experiences in an article in Phi Delta Kappan (June, 1999) written by Taron Wade. His WISE project was working at a local radio station.

> "WISE reinvents senior year. It teaches responsibilities and communication skills and opens their eyes to the real world.... I had a sense of doing something of value.... It's a transformative experience. What could

be better at bridging the gap between high school and whatever comes next than a program stressing self motivated learning."?

I don't know anything that better prepares high school seniors for college and work than WISE. Success at college and work depends on a number of academic skills, and so called "soft skills" like time management, organization, and communication without fear. WISE provides more basic, critical thinking and maturation skills than sitting in a classroom preparing for standardized multiple-choice tests. It is simply the best high school reform movement I have been involved in.

I now work for WISE Services, the non-profit organization that helps schools around the country establish and maintain similar programs. It is still my passion, 27 years after being introduced to it. It may not be new, but it is certainly more innovative, creative, and fresh than most of what is passing for reform these days.

CHAPTER 4:

ON TEACHING BOYS:

THE CHILD IS THE FATHER OF THE MAN

My son was born in 1990. By the time he was approaching kindergarten, we had to decide if he was to be one of those male kindergarten redshirts, held back a year to "mature." We decided against it. He was a very bright and very tall boy. We felt holding him back would, indeed, hold him back. What happened was eye- opening. In preschool and kindergarten, teachers thought he was "hyperactive." My wife is a clinical psychologist. She and I knew better. He was a boy. He acted differently than our daughter from his earliest, human moments. Eventually, we were proven right. He did fine in school. He was constantly described as very mature. A top student and athlete, he has been accepted to Tulane Medical School as I write this.

During the 1990s, a great deal of emphasis had been placed on improving the education of girls. Books like *Reviving Ophelia*, the work of Carol Gilligan, and the political pressure placed on policy makers by organizations such as the National Organization of Women (NOW) made girls' education a top reform of the early and mid-1990s. Much of this was very important and good policy. We worked hard on that reform, had workshops, read the research, and changed classroom behaviors to allow girls to be more assertive and improve their work. It was all good.

One afternoon in 1995, we had one of our monthly faculty conferences. It was on the subject of female experiences in the school, under the guise of "gender issues." At the long table sat several female students, and, at the far end, one male, Andrew. Andrew was last to speak. He was not one of the many superstar students. Andrew was an average kid who felt he had to speak up and tell the story from the male perspective. What Andrew had to say was a far cry from what most of us had heard, but some of his experiences rang true to me. What he said was that most boys don't have it as good in school here as "you all" think. He gave several examples. They sounded like what my son had experienced. Questions and comments came forth from a few interested people. One person, Ron Bouchier, the school's athletic director, came prepared. One of the issues discussed was male dominance in several areas, including sports. Ron not only disputed that, he presented sixteen years worth of evidence from team, league, sectional, state championships, finalist results, and even national, individual honors. The facts diametrically opposed the impression most of us had and clearly refuted what had been presented.

I was hooked. I knew Andrew and Ron to be straight shooters. They were on to something real and important. The trouble was that they were ignored at best, cynically assaulted at worse. I also knew the issues and stereotyping my son had gone through so far in school. I was determined to find out more. I started small. First, I looked closely at the grades of my senior students. I had no idea what I would find. Little did I know it would launch me on a sixteen-year investigation on the issues plaguing boys in schools.

A couple of years later, I was one of three Scarsdale staff members to go to a conference on boys held at Wellesley College. I was the only teacher. The other two (women) were an assistant superintendent and a guidance counselor, both members of the district's "Gender Equity Committee." It had already become obvious to me that *gender* was a euphemism for "Female Equity." While in a workshop on boys, I heard volumes about the problems of female students being harassed and bullied and intimidated by aggressive boys who needed to be "fixed." A bit nervous about presenting a different view, I stood up and recited a summary of what I had learned over the past few years of investigation in my school and from reading the local papers about valedictorians and salutatorians in Westchester County. After much criticism and claims I must be fabricating evidence, I was summarily dismissed. However, a woman sitting near me asked me to tell her more and also asked if I wouldn't mind being interviewed for a book she was writing. I said sure, and found the following in her book and article that appeared in the May 2000 edition of the *Atlantic Monthly*:

> Three years ago, Scarsdale High School in New York State held a gender-equity workshop for its faculty. It was the standard girls-are-being-shortchanged fare, with one notable difference: a male student gave a presentation in which he pointed to evidence suggesting that girls at Scarsdale High were well ahead of boys. David Greene, a social studies teacher, thought the student must be mistaken. But when he and some colleagues analyzed department grading patterns, they saw that the student was right. They found that in Advanced Placement social studies classes, there was little or no difference in grades between boys and girls. But in standard classes, the girls were doing a lot better. Greene also learned from the school's athletic director that its girls' sports teams were far more successful in competition with other schools than the boys' teams were. Of the twelve athletes from Scarsdale High named as All-American in the previous ten years, for example, three had been boys, nine [had been] girls. Greene came away with a picture flatly at odds with the administrators' preconception: one of ambitious girls and relatively disaffected boys who were willing to settle for mediocrity.
>
> Like schools everywhere, Scarsdale High has been strongly influenced by the girl-crisis climate. The belief that girls are systematically deprived prevails on the school's Gender Equity Committee; it is the rationale for the school's offering a special senior elective class on gender equity. Greene has tried gingerly to broach the subject of male underperformance with his colleagues. Many of them concede that in the classes they teach, the girls seem to be doing better than the boys, but they do not see this as part of a larger pattern. After so many

years of hearing about the silenced, diminished girls, the suggestion that boys are not doing as well as girls is not taken seriously even by teachers who see it with their own eyes in their own classrooms. (Summers 2001)

What had I found? In my classes, the boys' final grades were anywhere from three to five points lower than the girls'. Overall, that meant the difference between a B- and B or B+. When I checked other social studies classes, the pattern held. In Advanced Placement (AP) classes, there were no significant differences. A colleague of mine, John Harrison, and I researched grades from all subjects in the school. The patterns held, except in two or three of the highest-level science and math classes. I redid the work of Ron Bouchier and verified the information he had given those few years earlier. In fact, the pattern stayed the same. Together, John and I looked at all kinds of information. We followed the class of 2002 and found that in each year, approximately two-thirds of the bottom third of the class were boys and two-thirds of the top third were girls. This corresponded to the almost 3:1 ratio of girls to boys as valedictorians and salutatorians in the county of Westchester.

John and I presented our findings to the staff, and again, seven years later, they were hard-pressed to acknowledge what we had found. Not much had changed. Then, as part of an ongoing series of talks and forums for parents, the Scarsdale PT Council sponsored a forum on boys called, Are We Failing Our Boys? I had invited two other speakers with lots of letters following their names to give the talk what I thought would be more "cred." The expected audience was about thirty to fifty people. Two hundred and fifty people (almost entirely moms) showed up, and they were most interested in what I had to say about boys in Scarsdale. Mothers knew what was going on. So did I. But few are willing to acknowledge it in an academic world dominated by NOW and women studies at the university level.

I joined others in this work. I read a great deal on the subject. I gathered much information and from that work, teamed with Dr. Ed Stephens of the On Step Institute and Foundation for Male Studies, helped write a grant for the Leadership Learning Lab of the Central Park Historical Society, and spoke at Dominican College and the College Of New Rochelle.

THE NUMBERS SPEAK:

One of the most consistent findings in the research is that over the past thirty years, schools have moved to teaching methods that favor how girls learn. Add this to the increasing data about how boys are faring less and less well in school, and you have an understanding about how much of a crisis this is within education, especially among minority males, our most failing demographic.

What follows is a summary of what I have found over the years:

IN 2002:

Twelth-graders below basic literacy in reading tests:

MALES: 33%   FEMALES: 20%

Twelth-graders with a parent who graduated from college who scored below basic writing proficiency levels:

MALES: 27%   FEMALES: 9%

IN 2003:

70 percent of public high school students graduated
Of those,

- 72 percent of all female students

- 65 percent of all male students (-7%)

- 59 percent of African-American female students

- 48 percent of African-American male students (-11%)

- 58 percent for Hispanic female students

- 49 percent of Hispanic male students (-9%)

(Jay P. Greene and Marcus A. Winters, Manhattan Institute for Policy Research, civic report, No. 48, April 2006)

IN 2005:

BS degrees by age and gender

AGE	MALE	FEMALE
65 or higher	24.3%	14%
45-64	30.7%	26.6%
35-44:	29%	26.6%
25-34	27.2%	32.5%

(US Census: American Fact Finder)

IN 2008:

- **137** women have graduated college for every 100 men

- **130+** women earned master's degrees for every 100 men

  (National Center for Education Statistics)

IN 2010:

- **185** women have graduated from college for every 100 men

  (According to the Bureau of Labor Statistics,David Brooks, The New York Times)

ASIDE FROM THOSE COMPARATIVE ANNUAL STATISTICS, IN GENERAL, FROM K-12:

- Boys are greatly outnumbered in every extracurricular activity outside of sports, from student government to student newspapers and academic clubs.

- By twelve years of age, boys are almost twice as likely to have repeated at least one grade.

- Boys comprise the majority of permanent high school dropouts.

- Boys are approximately three times as likely to be diagnosed with ADHD or ADD.

- Boys are ten times as likely to be referred for possible ADHD/ADD as girls.

- Boys (ages fifteen to nineteen) are five times as likely as girls to commit suicide.

- Boys are more than twice as likely to be suspended from school.

- Boys are more than three times as likely to be expelled from school.

- Preschool boys (ages three to four) are expelled at a rate about four and a half times that of girls.

The US Department of Education concedes that no serious research is available comparing different instructional methods that might help boys. Many education researchers have been found to be reluctant regarding research aimed at exploring gender differences in learning. In short, the researchers have found that because of changes in the educational system, the average boy of fifty to seventy-five years ago would have been very likely diagnosed with ADHD today, especially if they were bored and gifted boys (Armstrong 1996; Hartnett et al. 2004; Howard and James 2003).

HOW DID THIS HAPPEN?

There is also a great deal of agreement on the major reasons why these horrors are occurring. Over the past twenty years, a great deal of knowledge has been accrued regarding biological and brain differences between boys and girls. Some of it shows the following: The language area of an average five-year- old boy's brain is the same as a three-and-a-half-year-old girl's, thus less able to learn to read in K-2 (NIMH 2006). Girls have more brain area in the frontal lobes devoted to language and expression of emotion, as well as superior connectors between language areas to the amygdala, the brain's emotional center (Neu 2007, 8).

Girls' advanced prefrontal cortex also provides an advantage in decision making and impulse control (Baron-Cohen 2003). Girls' brains process emotional (tend/befriend) tendencies at an earlier age, while boys rely more on the brain stem and cerebellum, resulting in more fight/ flight tendencies under stress (Taylor et al. 2000). Boy behavior is far more likely to be determined by Nietzsche's "will to power" (wanting to be in control of one's environment), thus more likely to turn to video games and exhibit more confrontational and contradictory behaviors (Gleitman 1980). As a result of this differentiated development of boy and girl brains, boys are worse listeners, and thus have greater difficulties in classrooms.

Other researchers point more directly at early academics in K-2. Boys are not as reading/writing ready as girls. This has led to higher stress and failures, producing diminishing boys' motivation. Oddly, or not, the nation that scores highest in the most widely used international reading and writing tests is Finland. They start formal school at the age of seven. Verbally structured classrooms tend to decrease motivation and performance of boys. The results show an increase in the use of boys' resting brain states, poor note taking, poor attention to directions, and less homework done. These results were especially found in middle and high schools with boys who had higher IQ scores and had earlier successes in elementary school (Gurian 2005, 246). (Hey...that was me, grades nine to eleven!) Often too, the boredom of bright boys is misdiagnosed as ADHD (Howard and James 2003).

Other educational mismatches between methods and gender differences abound. Overall changes in educational format and curricula over the past thirty years have been detrimental to boys' learning. Among these are: more reading and writing at earlier ages, less physical and non-linear learning, and the disappearance of gym and recess. The evidence shows that more schools have become less and less oriented to these boy strengths. Boys simply learn better when interested and motivated. The research has also shown that boys are primarily visual, logical, musical, kinesthetic, and naturalistic learners (James 2007, 228).

All the research points to the fact that boys simply learn better through experiential doing ("kenntnis") than learning about something through reading, whether print or computer-screen based ("wissenschaft"). Historically, boys' learning has gone from physical apprenticeships, action, and practice to sitting in verbal/ written learning environments (Grossman and Grossman 1994). The result is that normal fidgeting and physical movement, once necessary and normal, are now liabilities (Gurian 2005, 53). There are ways of reforming schools to take these issues into account, but they are not part of the No Child Left Behind syndrome.

Let's take MATH and English Language Arts (ELA). Over the years, even math problems have become more word oriented, for which girls' brains are believed to have an advantage. ELA is theme based and often revolves around character feelings. Boys are more analytical and think more in terms of plot and action. Girls see more global outcomes and themes (Jonassen and Grabowski 1993). Sax and Judith Kleinfeld (White House Conference on Helping American Youth, 2006) contend that although the basic drilling for elementary reading skills works through fourth grade, the ELA curricula and practices in grades four through twelve have contributed to poorer boys' results in those grades. In fact, although the test results of fourth-grade boys had improved, the twelfth-grade results show that one in four boys does not read at a basic level of proficiency, as opposed to one in sixteen girls (USDE 2007).

Another area to revisit is the issue of stereotyping. It is what got me interested in this issue in the first place. My son was stereotyped from an early age. Boys get the message that "typical boy behavior—loud, competitive, and physical--is bad, and that they need to become more like girls—quiet, cooperative, and gentle" (James 2007, 115). "Typical boy behavior" is often misdiagnosed as ADHD. According to both Michael Gurian and Leonard Sax, this occurs especially when the teacher first suggests ADHD testing. Sax postulates that occurs because most classroom settings are not boy-friendly enough; most teachers (predominantly female in the early grades) are not fluent in the needs of boys; and too many K-1 classrooms are inappropriately, academically advanced. (Ironically, since the early 1990s, girls have been getting the message to become more assertive, competitive, and more physical.)

In another example of stereotyping, a 1992 study showed that "60 percent of teachers believed that their male African-American students would not go on to college." In that particular study, 65 percent of the teachers surveyed were African-American (Garibaldi 1992). One reason was the sub-cultural "call and response" (Schwartz 2001; Townsend 2000) style of many inner-city males; physically active, loud, engaged, and enthusiastic learning is often perceived as angry and hostile (Grossman and Grossman 1994). Most upper-middle-class secondary schools (where many teachers come from) stress higher, critical-thinking skills, conceptual thinking, and applications, while most lower-socioeconomic, secondary schools, stress safety, class management, and rote learning to achieve success on basic skills, as shown on national standardized tests.

That is the reform that needs to be made most. The so- called DOE, NCLB, RTTT, reform movement, as it now stands, simply makes the situation regarding the education of boys even worse. The result is a lack of practice in the deeper understanding of material and the underlying skills for advancement, both to and in college. Today's "reforms" have led to more competent mediocrity in inner-city schools. Whatever the causes, boys are found with:

- Poorer motivation (Gurian 2005, 244)

- Poorer learning while sedentary, as a result of their need to move around (Gurian, Sax, James, Tyre, Neu, and others)

- Poorer ability to hear softer, higher sounds, such as female voices (McFadden 1998, and others)

- Poorer episodic memory, less oriented to detail, thus poorer at test taking (Davis 1999, and others)

- Poorer at planning and paying attention (Naglieri and Rojahn 2001)

- Poorer at delaying gratification (Canada 1999, 2000)

- Poorer emotional, communication skills

- A greater need for lists, clear directions, depth of learning vs. breadth (Gurian 2005, 48,)

- Greater frustration, with less control, and more discipline problems

- Greater use of the brain's "rest state" (zoning out or looking distracted)

- A preference to shut down or say they didn't do the work, instead of admitting they don't know (Gurian 2005,165)

WHAT CAN WE CHANGE?

How can we learn from all the research and institute real reform, beyond the Gates, Bloomberg, Duncan, and Rhee style we are currently engulfed by?

DISTRICTS CAN:

- Use more "kenntnis" (experiential learning) and less "wissenschaft" (the linear pursuit of knowledge).

- Install appropriate experiential learning programs in K-12.

- Restore old-fashioned kindergarten.

- Start formal school a year later. Both genders will benefit.

- Start middle school and high school at 9:00 am. Use adolescent sleep studies.

- Evaluate and improve the screening for ADHD.

- Use more effective modes of discipline. Boys, again, unlike girls, usually react better to "power assertion" (clearly stating the rules and explaining how they were broken) and "attention withdrawal" techniques, as opposed to induction (How would you feel if you were Johnny?). Induction, because it is not direct, often creates anger and defensiveness, and thus makes some boys suspicious over time, thus escalating their reactions (Heyman and Legare 2004).

- Provide access to good male mentors, heroes, and role models.

- Get parents and the community involved.

- Restore recess, and add more physical education classes...Jim needs Gym!

- Consider single-sex classrooms, subjects, or schools. (The research is inconclusive.)

TEACHERS CAN

- Use differentiated instruction and assessments based on boys' preferred learning styles and intelligences. As math has included more word problems and essay questions (female strengths), ELA and social studies should incorporate questions allowing for visual answers (e.g., cartooning), and grade for logic and being concise.

- Design units and lessons using Grant Wiggins *Understanding by Design* (1998). Start at the outcomes and plan backward, including appropriate, authentic assessments.

- Provide reading choices. Boys comprehend more when they read about their interests.

- Questions should ask, what would you "do"? as opposed to, what would you "feel"?

- Use analogies where possible. It is a boy strength...either as a teaching tool or in tests. (So why did the College Board remove these from SAT tests?)

- Give problem-solving assignments.

- Use direct language in giving directions. Be matter of fact. Do not coddle. Give them what they need in order to solve the problem.

- Be vigilant about monitoring work and returning results swiftly and constructively.

- Train students to take verbatim notes and then to summarize them.

- Use voice modulation so boys can hear well.

- Add touch and eye contact, depending on subcultural issues.

- Use visuals, graphics, art, drama, music, and physical activities.

- Build in strategic "brain breaks."

- Use humor.

- Use competition, with winners and losers, especially as part of a team.

- Put boys in groups larger than three.

- Do not over-compliment boys or sweeten comments without merit. Self-esteem for boys must be addressed differently than for girls. Boys, unlike girls, will not do better if they think they are good in a subject (Baumeister et al. 2003).

The Gates, Bloomberg, Duncan, and Rhee, TFA, and Teachers College Workshop model reform movement have thrown many of these methods out. It's time we looked back at the research and matched up our classroom activities with the findings.

- "If you think about how many boys are getting bad grades, failing tests, not performing in class, becoming discipline problems—and if you look beyond the reading and writing gap, you might notice other key elements of male nature that are now a mismatch with conventional schooling" (Gurian 2005, 52).

- "Despite the research, schools that allow boys to function in accordance with their natural development are a dying breed" (Tyre 2008, 75).

- Many school districts, from Atlanta to Wilmette, have finally realized they must react to these issues. In Wilmette, after a huge, districtwide probe, a "final committee report provided irrefutable evidence that [even] upper-middle-class boys were not thriving in school." The Board of Education's response "was clear: Do whatever it takes to improve the performance of all children—including boys" (Tyre 2008, 121,122).

Thus, it is our task to create a more equitable education system for boys, without sacrificing the success of its girls. To accomplish this, all involved must open their minds beyond the current trends and understand the research-based, socio- neurobiological foundations of cognitive gender differences as they relate to education. We must recognize the levels to which curricula and teaching respond or fall short in relation to these research-based foundations. And we must develop educational approaches based on solid research to provide a more boy-friendly instructional climate, yet still be responsive to both genders (James 2007, 8).

CHAPTER 5:

THE ART OF TEACHING

GREAT TEACHING IS ART

What follows is what I, and many others have learned over the years and would use to mentor new or less experienced teachers. These tips are just as good for a, boss, parent, or coach. Each teaches others in some way. Examine each suggestion carefully. Adapt. Bend. Use them to germinate your own ideas, or steal them outright. There are no copyright rules to good techniques or good ideas. If it isn't a fit, the first to know will be the students, and they will lose all respect for that teacher. They don't abide "fronters" well. The same is true of employees, children, or players.

Great teaching is an art, not to be controlled and censored by scientific management. For example, what do good teachers do those first days? There are no hard and fast rules. Some believe in getting right to work. However that is only possible if the students already are captives of the school culture: If they already know what to do and how to do it and if they are motivated by grades and getting into the best schools. However, even under those circumstances, usually it's been two months since kids have done anything. How eager are they for school? They haven't met their new teachers yet. They are either nervous about how they will be perceived, anxious about how hard the class will be, or looking as the teacher as "fresh meat". As a result, wise teachers take a day or two to introduce them to expectations, the grading system, the class methodology, and some of the really cool stuff you plan to do with them. Good teachers often sell the class.

In poor, inner-city schools, where kids are code switching (code switching, as defined by Elijah Anderson in his 1999 book, *Code Of The Street*, means to speak the linguistic and sociological languages of the street and of the wider society) or are not captivated by the school culture, teachers cannot simply start the curriculum, no matter how much pressure there is to get prepared for tests. As soon as their new teacher walks in the door, they are passing judgment. Champ or chump? Hard or soft? For us or against us? Condescending or caring? Teachers have to show students they are "hard," yet caring, champs.

CODE SWITCHING

One thing we all have to do is learn to be able to code switch. This is most true for teachers in "tough" schools. "You have to be tough. If you show fear, others will exploit it." Too often, though, teachers unfortunately mistake authoritarianism for toughness (as do obnoxious cops and administrators) and thus fail to "respect to be respected." In that case, kids, even young ones, will take on an oppositional role, and you will have done nothing but add fuel to the fire. On the other hand, a teacher that shows fear is done. "Put a fork in her." Show fear, and you are vulnerable to being undone.

A few tips from Nicolo Machiavelli might come into play here. (Not everything Machiavelli wrote should be taken negatively. Many famous–as well as infamous–leaders, have wisely followed these words.) The code of the street and the code of politics in his era are not too dissimilar:

- To understand the nature of the people, one must be a prince, and to understand the nature of the prince, one must be of the people.

- He who wishes to be obeyed must know how to command.

- It is better to be feared than loved, if you cannot be both.

- Benefits should be conferred gradually; and in that way, they will taste better.

- It should be understood that there are two types of fighting: one with laws and the other with force... but it often happens that the first is not enough, which requires that we have recourse to the second.

- Since it is necessary for the prince to use the ways of beasts, he should imitate the fox and the lion, because the lion cannot defend himself from snares, and the fox cannot defend himself from wolves. Therefore, it is important to be a fox in order to understand the snares and a lion in order to terrify the wolves. Those who choose only to be a lion do not really understand. (Nicolo Machiavelli 1513)

With those phrases in mind, the job is to learn the code of the street and teach the culture of the school. Teachers have to learn how not to be taken advantage of and how to have kids maintain their respect for them. In each class, they must create a critical mass of kids on their side. How they use the tools, inspire, excite, respect who they are, and motivate, will all determine that.

Good teachers teach expectations. They let students know they can do well, how they are expected to, and how they will earn their grades. They explain what will be happening in class, both the dull and exciting, without B---S. Good teachers are honest and forthright. They take nothing for granted, but aren't condescending. Good teachers make expectations are both oral and written with the written version in the front of student's notebooks. It is a good idea for these expectations to be contractual, signed by teacher, student, and parents. Everyone knows what is expected, with their positive and negative sanctions.

Having a sense of humor helps. Regardless of what every teacher may have heard about sarcasm, especially in many urban classes, it is part of the code switching you have to do. The best teachers often have to be able to "do the dozens" to survive.

(According to *Urban Dictionary*, doing the dozens is an African-American custom in which two competitors--usually males--go head-to-head in a competition of comedic trash talk. They take turns "cracking on," or insulting, one another, their adversary's mother, or other family members, until one of them has no comeback.)

Self-esteem is a whole different thing here. You have to be concerned with yours, too. In the words of "Rastaman the Griot" from the movie *Bulworth*, "You got to be a spirit! You can't be no ghost."

The best teachers know they will continually have to teach and reteach those expectations, skills, and methods, especially if they are literally foreign to many kids. They must remember how their students must learn to become bilingual, to code switch between street and school languages and cultures. More importantly, the most significant part of teaching is to teach children, not just to do the right things, but to do the right thing *right*, for the *right* reasons.

When you give a direction, what do you expect? You expect everyone to follow the directions. Imagine being a coach. You call a play, and only two-thirds of your team runs that play. A class is a team. In this regard, they are not a group of individuals. Everyone has to be on the same page. Everyone has to acknowledge leadership. If not, teachers have lost control of the classroom and will spend more time "managing" than teaching.

But you can't be mean, cruel, intimidating, or draconian you say. You don't have to be. In fact, you shouldn't be...unless, from time to time, you have no choice. There is a difference between being authoritarian and the authority figure. This is a part of the class culture teachers must create. Using positive, crisp, firm, demonstrative statements that fit their personality will allow them to have their students act in a disciplined manner... doing the right thing the right way.

For example, if a teacher first asks students to take out their notebooks and do something assumed they know how to do, that teacher has made it harder on herself. In the beginning of the year, until students are used to the routine, each step has to be done separately to assess each step. Slow down. If the expectation is to have them automatically doing that to get the period going, what do you do if 90 percent are doing it? Is that good enough to make it the expected behavior? No. If you leave the door open now to 10 percent noncompliance, you have created the atmosphere that will lead to 10 percent compliance later. That will only increase. Then, when you are sure all notebooks are out, start them on the task for a precise amount of time. It shouldn't take long for them to know and follow the procedure, so that you can combine both tasks into one.

ONLY IF YOU MEAN IT.

In the beginning of the year, good teachers plan for reinforcement time. This is in addition to the necessary time for explaining and modeling the tasks students are expected to internalize. It is the time for repetition as sanctioning. Neither positive, nor negative, repetition is simply a means to an end. Students must understand that these sanctions are not punishment. Repetition is a memory tool. The more often we correctly do something, the faster we establish muscle and brain memory that makes that activity routine. This must be explained to kids, who are more than likely to question why they have to do something again. You have to tell them why they are repeating entering the room. It goes back to getting 100 percent of the details right 100 percent of the time. Doing this from the beginning of the school year leads to an established entry and class routine. You will rarely have to spend time on it later in the year, thus maximizing class time for the rest of the year.

Many veteran teachers use the expression, "Never let them see you smile until Christmas." This isn't to be taken literally. The idea is that a teacher must become a leader whose first task is to establish control of the expectations, not control of the students. Control of the expected behavior is what makes a classroom work. If you have to take acting classes to make this work, it's a good investment. Besides, being a thespian is always a good teacher trait. For your students to take you seriously, you must take your commands seriously and make sure all comply. If not, you spend your time trying to get kids to do what they should be doing, instead of getting them to learn what they should be learning.

SHOW TIME

Ever act? Sing in public? Do any public speaking? Teaching involves some of the same skills. Projection without yelling is very important. "From the diaphragm." "Eye contact." "Use your outside voice." Use your inside voice." "Modulate tone and pitch." "Posture." "Know your audience." "Make each person in the audience feel like you are talking only to them." "Purpose?" Each of these learnable skills must be part of your teaching technique.

In addition, Teachers have to plan how to train and use their voice. By this, I mean, that there is an ebb and flow to class dynamics. Teachers have to listen, as much or more, than speak. They have to know when *not* to speak. For example, never to talk while others talk. (You don't want any of your classroom speakers doing that, either.) Teachers model public speaking. If they want their kids to have meaningful discourse, they have to "show and tell" how. It is not done purely for classroom control.

Blocking is part of acting. Where and how actors are positioned on stage are often more important than the words that flow from their lips. Teaching is similar. Nonverbal communication is very important. Body language and facial gestures must match tone of voice. Lincoln, standing still and erect at the front of the room, raised his chin and announced clearly to the captivated throng.... Well, it doesn't matter what he said. I've got your attention already. You know his words will be historic. Would they have the same effect if the stage directions said, Lincoln, shifting nervously from one foot to another, turned sideways and lowered his eyes as he spoke to the crowd? Nope. There's a time for formal posing, and informal, as in...John sat at the edge of the desk, threw up his hands, and with an amazed look, quizzically said, "How did that other guy get to be president?"

Finally, regarding voice lessons, sometimes when we are most nervous, we must simply take a breath. Eli stopped before he spoke in the huddle. He took a deep breath, and without shouting, he clearly and succinctly called the next play after the loss of ten yards on the previous play. Again, think of stage directions. What emotional state do those directions imply, as opposed to this example? Frustrated by the huge loss on the previous play, Peyton ran to the huddle, gasped for air, and quickly mumbled the next play. Which QB would you prefer?

How, you ask, can a teacher do that? They must stop. Pause. Use the hairy eyeball. Show the "I am serious" look. Lower their voice half an octave. Then, say again what they want. They have to use the least invasive techniques first. Nonverbal gestures or facial expressions are great signals that don't cause a ruckus. They have to "Speak softly and carry a big stick." They must firmly, but without yelling, give a public, concise reminder of what students should be doing right at the start of noncompliance. Wait too long, and they are sunk.

Notice, there is no please. It is not a request. It is a command. Commands do not take away from being a nice person. Another common issue teachers often face is calling out. If a teacher has told students they will only call on those with raised hands, they must only call on those with raised hands. From the very first day of class, when a student calls out, he must be told to raise his hand, then call on someone who did it correctly. Often this happens because kids don't listen. They hear while waiting to be heard next. They must be reminded to "Check your eyes. Are they on the speaker?" Sometimes, your reminders will be more private. As you walk over to Donald, you might have to lean over and quietly say, "Donald, I need you to track the speaker with your eyes to read that person's lips. You know that will allow you to understand better. When I get back to the other side of the room, I will be watching you."

Other times, teachers may need to make a private statement more public to foster public compliance. By singling out one student, you can remind all to do what is right. "Theodore, look at Alvin while you speak louder, so Alvin can hear you." "Thank you, Theodore." "Alvin and the rest of this row, good tracking of Theodore while he speaks." Regardless of public or private, speed is imperative.

RULES OF ENGAGEMENT.

What if Alvin and Theodore don't comply? More important is the question teachers must ask themselves, "What will the rest of the class be like if I don't handle this well?" Because the long-term results are so important, what is done with Alvin and Theodore is a means to an end. This is where we heed Machiavelli's and Sun Tzu's advice. The incident is best handled quickly, quietly, and with the least disturbance. Regardless of how flustered teachers must stay cool, calm, and collected. Demeanor is most important. Solving the problem, without having to resort to extrinsic consequences, gives the most intrinsic power. However, if consequences are called for, it is important to think of "behavioral work" more like foreign policy. One must act quickly, non-emotionally, and with the least invasive consequence that works.

As a polished statesman has a series of steps in his portfolio, so must a successful teacher. Here is a flow chart, as recommended by Ari Rusila. Ok, a joke is a joke. There is, however, a series of escalating steps diplomats use to deal with "unfriendlies," short of the final step--war. We don't want war in the classroom. There are no winners. You may win a battle, but you will lose the war for "hearts and minds." (http://arirusila.wordpress.com/tag/cfsp/)

Those steps look something like this. Good diplomats start informally and only escalate when necessary. So, too, do good teachers.

WAR

Mobilize

Escalate Sanctions

Negotiate

Informal Talk

Let's examine a point too often overlooked; that is, bad behavior can't be overlooked. Many new teachers believe, erroneously, that the least invasive act is to ignore it. The paradox is that, in the long run, it is the most invasive. Ignore it, and you signal that bad behavior is ok. Then the "other side" will escalate, and, instead of efficiently and effectively nipping it in the bud, the teacher will be forced to escalate retaliation. We don't want to do that, do we? Remember, the purpose is not to gain or maintain power. The purpose is to have kids learn efficiently. To do that, they must comply with directions and instructions, whether written or oral. Language, tone, and demeanor cannot show a struggle for power. It must show concern and care for their learning.

For emphasis the good teacher must: First, stay cool. Be firm, calm, and collected. Second, move and observe. Call kids on what they do. Make sure they know they are being watched. Encourage them to see the speaker, who demands attention at that moment. Third, remind kids that partial compliance is not acceptable. Imagine "almost driving" on the right side of a two- way street. I don't think we want that. Fourth, and probably foremost, make conscious skills into unconscious skills. The goal, through persistence, is to allow students to gain the positive habits of mind and learning we want them to have to succeed throughout life.

HUH, WHAT DID YOU SAY?

We want our kids to learn how to learn. For those skills to become conscious, we can't assume they know what we know. As a result, when we want them to succeed at a task, we need to not only make sure they know what to do, but also how to do it. Directions, therefore, are *specific, clear, sequential,* and *observable* (Lemov 2010, 179).

Specific directions are concise and clear. They are easy to remember and clearly useful. As a result of good directions, kids never have to ask why they are doing something. It is infinitely clear because of the language you use. Only black-and-white directions are clear, regardless of the complexity of the tasks. Think of all the poorly worded instructions for using your new snow blower, smart phone, or new application, and then do the opposite when you write yours. (How are mine, by the way? Clear enough?)

Effective instructions are also sequential. Steps 1, 2, and 3 must be clear, not only in what they say, but the order they are in. For example, how much sense does this make?

1. Write the answers to the questions on the board.

2. Take out your notebook.

3. Sit down.

Finally, teachers must ensure kids are following the directions correctly. Directions must have a built-in means of accountability, either visual or otherwise. To do do this correctly means to write directions more concisely. For example, if a teacher wants his students to share work on the class Smart Board, he must say, "Moe, come to the front of the room... pause...Take a marker from the Smart Board.....pause... Answer the question on the top of the Board in the box with your name on it...pause... When you are done, put the marker back where you found it, and sit down in your seat."...pause...."Larry, when Moe is seated, you will do exactly as he did, except you will answer the question in the box marked Larry." .... pause... "Curly, just sit and watch, until it is your turn, and stop that 'woo, woo' noise now."

IT'S THE LITTLE THINGS.

Everyone loves a distraction once in a while, but we all have to be wary of getting off the topic. Once we set the direction for the conversation, one of the teacher's jobs is to keep the conversation focused and not allow students to "go off" on something else, unless it serves a good and timely purpose. Second, when having to talk to a student about a behavior issue, teachers must watch out for them turning the conversation away from where it is intended. For example, a teacher might have to stop class to say, "Alice, stop turning around to talk to Ralph." Alice (especially in middle school) will undoubtedly try to make Ralph the culprit (which he undoubtedly is), but that is a separate issue. She might say, "Ralph told me to go to the moon." That answer is irrelevant. The teacher must respond, "Alice, do not turn around. To understand the process we are trying to learn, you have to face forward and keep your eyes and ears on the speakers. Show me you will do that." Of course, in a short time, as you walk around the room, you will quietly approach Ralph and whisper in his ear, "Ralph, I heard you say 'To the moon, Alice,' and I expect you not to do that again, or we will discuss astronomy after school."

If you've noticed, you have read a great deal of detailed work, not so much as to bore you (I hope), but enough for you to see it's in the details, the little things. A few years ago, I made up T-shirts for the offensive linemen I coached. On the front had their Line's nickname, and on the back it said, "Details, details, details." Linemen never really get to make splashy scenes. They just do the grunt work to make the runners and throwers look great. That work, to be successful, is all in the details. They work those t-shirts with pride. Many authors have noted the incredible turnaround of New York City's quality of life. One of the generally, agreed-upon reasons for the turnaround was the police department's attack on the little things that sabotaged life. They went after graffiti artists, the windshield-washer guys, beggars, spitters, and the like. Lo and behold, dealing with those little details somehow created a change in the culture of New York City, and what behavior was tolerated and tolerable.

The lesson here is important. The little things count. As a coach, I continually emphasized those details from the very beginning of the preseason. One of our team goals was "100 percent of the details 100 percent of the time." This is the expectation. Not surprisingly, even from the most motivated teenager, at first, that percentage comes as a surprise. What percentage are they comfortable with? Have you asked them? You'd be surprised how far from 100 percent it is. However, when that goal is explained and discussed, they "get it." It must then be reinforced. If directions are not followed, they must do it again, and understand why it is important to get the details right. Over time it sticks. What works on the athletic field, can work in the classroom, if we are determined to have students "learn how to learn."

Neatness counts. If a teacher wants the seats to be in certain places, he must make sure they are there each day before class starts, and make sure the kids are instructed to put them back where they were. If that teacher wants class work and homework to be done a certain way (she should), then students must be shown how, and held accountable from the very beginning of the term. They should be provided a rubric that includes both positive and negative sanctions. If that teacher wants notebooks organized, students must be shown how as often as necessary with sanctions like a grade for organization.

A good teaching habit is to exaggerate for emphasis until what is expected becomes habit. How do we want them to work at their desks? Work in groups? Speak publicly? Do research? Take notes? Take tests? Write essays? Learn content? Comprehend reading? Increase vocabulary? Solve for x? Treat each other? Give presentations? The task doesn't matter. What matters is that they internalize the goal of 100 percent of the details 100 percent of the time for every task from the very beginning of the school year. The real goal in teaching is less about content and more about behavior modification. If we help them internalize how to learn, they will do better in all content areas.

BE DIFFERENT, JUST LIKE EVERYONE ELSE.

Not all techniques work for all teachers in all circumstances. One must be genuine. A teacher must create his own style, tone, and demeanor. I was initially taught when I was teaching in high school to begin each class at the door, to usher kids in the room and out of the hallway to show punctuality as an expected behavior. Eventually, I learned that each student might need a different kind of remark or encouragement as he or she entered. Different teachers use that opportunity to do a face-to-face hello with a handshake to reinforce manners, or hand out materials with a reminder to follow the directions. Sometimes it is just a warm smile that a student needs. That teacher must establish a procedure that is as regular as possible, fits his personality, sets tones and expectations, and gets thing started *on time*. Even if he can't get to the door because of a myriad of reasons, he must have an opening procedure that accomplishes what the greeting accomplishes and gets them transitioned to work ASAP. He has a period planned for *X* minutes, not *X* minus seven minutes. Every moment lost at the beginning is lost. There are few opportunities to "make up for lost time." The opportunity cost of not starting on time in the expected manner is the loss of a valuable idea, summary, discussion point, or fact.

Follow-up questions also allow teachers to *"differentiate."* It is more effective and efficient to differentiate by asking frequent, targeted, and challenging questions to the class. Traditional differentiation by breaking kids into ability groups stigmatizes kids. They know what it means to be in "this" group or "that" group. It also reinforces the behaviors that got them there in the first place. "Why bother? We're in the dummy group." Traditional differentiation into ability groups also makes teachers *work harder, not smarter*. (Working smarter, not harder, by the way, is a skill you need to learn and to model for kids who stress themselves out.)

The best questions ask how or why. If more kids need to respond that aren't up to that, teachers can ask who, what, where, and when. That's differentiation. In most subjects, especially in the humanities, there are questions that are subject to points of view. Ask for other points of view. Ask for alternative solutions to math problems. Ask for a better vocabulary word. Ask for evidence. Ask them to apply the answer to another problem or situation. My favorite question is, *"So what?"* That forces them to think about either the significance of an event, or the importance of understanding a concept. Not only does it break the tension, it allows the student to stop and think about the importance of what was said.

Good teachers become "bilingual." They learn vocabulary and speech rhythms to communicate effectively in the world of their students. At the same time good teachers make their students bilingual to communicate in the larger world. This is one of our most important tasks. Our students have to succeed, not only in their subculture, but also in the larger, American culture, and society. Good grammar in the classroom counts. The ability to use good grammar in other settings is part of code switching. If kids from the street can't code switch, they are forever doomed to stay where they are, no matter how smart and capable they are.

Here's something else that is an important part of the learning process: exact vocabulary. Vernacular or technical expressions that are essential for understanding any subject, trade, or profession are at the very core of success throughout life. I don't want to have surgery done on me by a doctor who calls my anterior cruciate ligament "that rubber band thingy" or the "arterial crucial logarithm."

EXPECT THE UNEXPECTED.

How can anyone plan reactions to the unexpected? Simple. Expect the unexpected, and know what you will do in case Jack takes out his "Stratocaster" and starts a "Black Sabbath" riff. This comes under no methodology heading. Who a teacher is will dictate how she will deal with Jack as quickly and effectively as possible. I would (depending on my knowledge of Jack as a person) either use humor to get him to stop, or directly command him to stop. It is based on who I am. I was seen as a funny yet intimidating person, a bit on the crazy side. Unpredictability can be a good thing. I might have asked him to give me the guitar so I could play something. Then, after the surprised Jack easily handed it over to me, I'd say, "I meant after class, when I will also give it back to you."

Various versions of this story actually happened. Once, I was walking down the hall in Stevenson High School and saw a kid smoking. When I walked up to him, I didn't yell; I didn't explode; I didn't act in any way threatening. I simply asked him for a drag. He gave the cigarette to me instantly. I put it out (on the wall for dramatic effect), reminded him that smoking was bad for him, as well as against school rules, and walked away. He stood there dumbfounded and later told his friends not to mess with "that crazy tall dude" when they saw me in the halls. I gained a "rep." Your "rep" defines you. How kids see you dictates how they react to your directions. You must establish your "rep" as you want it, as soon as you can. Word gets out, and when it does, it is very hard to reverse a "soft" rep.

Whatever one's rep, one must act quickly, give no warnings, be decisive, be appropriate (to the incident and its severity), and dispassionate. Time is of the essence. Warnings indicate softness. Decisiveness indicates strength. Appropriateness indicates fairness, as does a non-emotional response.

TOUGH BUT FAIR.

Whatever your personality, students must think of each teacher as being "tough, but fair." Mr. Jones may be funny, warmhearted, caring, strict, or any of the above, but must be thought of as "tough but fair." He can't be gotten over on, and he can't play favorites.

Often teachers do not see the difference in the cause of a student's "misbehavior." Misbehavior is simply not doing the right thing the right way. Why didn't Johnny "bang the drum slowly?" Did he bang it quickly because he felt like messing with the teacher, or did he not hear the directions? The first reason indicates noncompliance and that he was testing the authority figure. The second instance simply indicates that he wasn't following a basic procedure, the act of listening correctly. Perhaps he only heard bang the drum, and turned his ears off for the last word in his excitement. Or, was he half asleep because it is 8:00 am and had no sleep, because he sleeps with two brothers in the same bed who both snore? Or, did he bang it fast because he didn't understand what slowly meant? That is the teacher's fault. Did he demonstrate how slowly, slowly was? To someone used to pulsating music with 160 beats per minutes, 120 beats per minute is slowly. To someone who listens to cool jazz, 120 beats per minute is fast. A metronome would have worked. Most smart phones have an "app that does that."

If the reaction doesn't match the reason for the misbehavior, is the teacher being fair? *No!* She is simply being "unfair" (the most overused word in student vocabulary). Knowing why someone misbehaves dictates the level of response. Does it mean Mr. Jones (after noting his error) uses that metronome to model slowly, or privately walk over to Johnny and tell him why it is important to hear directions, or, if Mr. Jones knows he was being tested, have a reasonably scaled, set of consequences depending on a few factors. Is this the first time? To what extent is he being defiant? Increment the implementation of sanctions. First or lesser offenses call for lower-level responses (see the earlier diplomacy chart). Calmly, do the right thing the right way. Mr. Jones must model that and not to resort to calling for help. It is a signal of weakness. Save the biggest weapon for last or the most egregious actions. Does Johnny simply need to repeat the action correctly? Does he need to apologize to Mr. Jones or the class? Does he need a time-out? Does he need to come to Mr. Jones after class? After school? Whenever that is, public defiances must have a private conversation to get to the root of the problem and solve it face-to-face. It is Mr. Jones' time to counsel and become a trusted ally, not a foe.

"I COME TO BURY CAESAR, NOT TO PRAISE HIM"

Shakespeare's *Julius Caesar* teaches us that false praise encourages bad actions. When people are overpraised for doing good, they believe they are great. When they get false praise for doing something less than correctly, they think they did it correctly. If they are praised for mediocrity, they think they are good enough. It leads students to incorrectly think they are meeting expectations.

If wrongly used, praise can bury a teacher. Mr. Jones must know the how acknowledgment and praise differ so that he acknowledges when expectations have been met and praises exceptional work. Doing anything else is disingenuous and condescending. What message do we send by overenthusiastically praising Julius for simply taking out his notebook. ("That was a fabulous job of taking your notebook from your backpack, Julius.") Julius knows that his action was not fabulous at all. What he thinks is that you are a B.S., goody-goody who thought so little of him that you didn't think he could do such a simple task. In addition, according to Doug Lemov (2010, 211), research shows "that students have come to interpret frequent praise as a sign that they are doing poorly and need encouragement from their teachers. They see cheap praise as a marker of failure, not success." At the same time, they have lost respect for the teacher whose words are not true or meaningful.

Everything teachers do and say in the classroom is more than subject teaching. They mold young hearts, minds, and psyches. "Clear eyes, strong hearts, can't lose" is the team motto of the Dillon Panthers of the book, movie, and TV series, *Friday Night Lights*. Students must develop clear eyes to see those expectations and the methods and techniques to reach them. They must have strong hearts to withstand failures and have the courage to meet challenges. With both, they know they "can't lose," even with the odds stacked against them. What they won't lose is self-esteem, because it has been developed by achievement, not by false praise intended to do so.

There is good praise. Good praise recognizes self-correction. It recognizes the achievement of something within the student's control. It recognizes that a student has accomplished what he couldn't do, couldn't do as well, or reaches the next level. Good praise recognizes good work habits that will enable the student to accomplish a goal again and again, thus building on his accomplishment.

There is also good criticism. Somewhere along the line, we became so infatuated (without longitudinal research) with self-esteem that teachers were told not to criticize work because it would hurt students' feelings, and, therefore, their self-esteem. We were told to be their friends and confidants. Constructive criticism became anathema in some circles. Thus, Mr. Jones began to praise work simply because a student tried. What did that teach kids? It taught many to put on a phony face, look like they were working hard, when they really weren't, and let them think they beat the system. What good habits were created? Zippo, and I don't mean the lighter. (Does anyone remember Zippo lighters?)

Getting the student from "I don't know", or not trying, to find the right answer, builds better self-esteem. We cannot allow students to "opt out," as Nemov puts it, by the use of false praise.

If a student doesn't answer, or says, "I don't know," another student who does know should be asked for the answer, the first should repeat it. Quickly. Ms. Smith cannot get locked in a duel. If a student's answer is weak, Ms. Smith should ask him probing questions that help her discover the answer and have other students augment the original answer. The goal is to get the excellent answer, not the one that is half right. What example are you setting if Ms. Smith settles for a half right answer? What does it say about what Ms. Smith believes about their abilities?

If students don't answer correctly, they can't be falsely complimented. Tests and future employers won't falsely pass or hire them. They must know that right is right. If they are almost right, honesty is important. "Julius, that is almost right." Probing questions then help them figure out the rest. We cannot ever confuse effort with excellence, unless we want them to. Praise the effort, and help students work toward excellence.

There are several ways to do this. Versions of, "Can you add to that?" or repeating with emphasis the incorrect portion of the response can trigger the right response. If a student has tried to take the easy way out by answering another question (commonly kids give an example or synonym, instead of an explanation for what you really asked), say so. "Irving, I didn't ask for an example of a revolution. I asked what might cause one."

Sometimes, they answer the question they figured was to be asked next in a sequence because they knew that one. So, you have to respond. "Cleopatra, I asked what that last portion of the experiment demonstrated, not what will we do next." The key here is that kids learn that process is as important as product. Correct processes can be used over and over again in different subjects and circumstances at all ages through adulthood.

To really establish self-esteem, challenge students to expand on an answer. Pull a Star Trek. Have them "boldly go where [they have not] gone before." Follow up questions challenge students to show understanding, not just memorization. Have you ever seen the smile on a kid who answered a question he never even thought he could understand? Then imagine how he feels about himself when you walk over and fist bump (or whatever the newest, latest thing is). *This is why we are here.* If we can accomplish this with a critical mass, the tide has turned toward the class and school culture we expect.

I AM NOT YOUR BUDDY.

A friend (now) who has been teaching successfully at a Bronx high school for the past several years was a student of mine in 1986. Ms. Gong (a pseudonym) and her friend pranced into my first class in this school on that fateful September day. These two sophomores thought--as do most students with a bit of spunk--here's the new teacher...let's see what he has. I was new to them, but I already had sixteen-years experience in a school far tougher than theirs. When it was clear that I was not going to let them get away with their antics during class, and told them to see me in the adjoining office following class, they were annoyed. When they tried to make me back down, I stopped them and lit into them firmly, yet without yelling.

Ms. Gong cried. After offering her a tissue, we talked more about what happened and ended the incident with my saying, "now you know what I expect." She became one of my best students and thanked me for showing her that I cared so much for her that I stood up to her antics. Her prior teachers had given in and therefore given up on her. When I visited her in her school this past year, it was obvious how much she was loved, respected, and feared by the tough, teenage boys who towered over her. I asked a couple of them why. They responded that she loved them and showed it by challenging them to achieve higher expectations of behavior, not just test results. She turned to me and told them, "See him? He is why. He did the same to me. He even made me cry in tenth grade." So they all came up and shook my hand, "and we had a great time on the [group W] bench, talkin' about...all kinds of groovy things that we was talking about on the bench." (With thanks to Arlo Guthry, "Alice's Restaurant.")

Teachers are not students' friends. Teachers are guides, facilitators, mentors, distributors of knowledge, and even counselors, but not friends--at least not until after graduation. In work with students, teachers have to be both caring and strict. Nemov (2010, 213) accurately says we "must be both: caring, funny, warm, concerned, and nurturing--and also strict, by the book, and sometimes inflexible." Caring and strictness are the Yin and Yang of the student-teacher relationship. Together they are one.

When I taught at Scarsdale High School, we gave out teacher evaluation forms each term (a good idea if done right). After tabulation, I would print-up and share the results with each class. Invariably, they laughed when they saw it. I titled it *Dr. Jekyll and Mr. Hyde.* Although my rating as a teacher was consistently very high, for most of the questions, about half the class saw the same actions as being either too strict or really caring. After a good laugh, we discussed what that meant. Lincoln knew "you can fool some of the people all of the time, and all of the people some of the time, but you cannot fool all of the people all of the time." As a teacher, one cannot fear being strict or caring. However teachers should fear being *disingenuous.*

Kids understand language. They know the difference between criticizing behavior and demeaning them. they have to hear that what they did was incorrect, not that they are stupid. Stupid is a funny word. People aren't stupid. Actions are. People are ignorant. For example, I am absolutely ignorant about nuclear medicine. I, however, am not stupid. For years, I taught kids the subtle differences. I gave them my definition of stupidity. I am not sure where this idea came from, but I surely will pass it along. While Ignorance is simply not knowing or not knowing better, *"Stupidity is the act of knowing what to do, when to do it, and then choosing not to."* When working with kids of all ages (even adults), we need to know the difference. In doing so, we have to distinguish between the act and the actor, make sure the actor knows what to do, acts humanly and humanely, and be ourselves as we do all that. We must not be afraid of criticizing stupidity while building confidence to meet great expectations.

CLASSROOM CONVERSATION IS PUBLIC SPEAKING

The next issues involved in good communication are the dual arts of speech and hearing. Kids who answer questions in a class of twenty-five are speaking publicly. They have to be taught how. They need to learn to make eye contact; they need to learn to speak audibly, so that the person farthest from them in the room clearly hears them. Teachers need to move around the room to become that farthest person. We need to use one-word commands, like "voice," or nonverbal commands, like ear-tugging or hand-pointing to the ceiling to indicate that the speaker must be louder. We need to tell the student sitting next to us to ask the speaker to speak up because he or she can't hear.

At the same time, we have to train the class how to listen. They must be told repeatedly to "read lips" and track the speaker's mouth with their eyes. Many studies have shown greater aural understanding when doing so, as compared to looking elsewhere. It teaches them the art of focus.

Games like "Simon Says" teach them to "stay in the moment" and that listening depends on seeing, too.

Also important to communication in a classroom is the sociological concept of space. How a room is laid out, its seating arrangement, says a lot about what kind of communication you expect and want. Trendy, group tables produce the very distractions you are trying to prevent. Groups at tables should be just for group work; they don't help individual or quiet work. Separate, movable desks that can be rearranged for different kinds of class work allow for far more flexibility. The following arrangement is often used:

This works for some lessons if *space* is left for Ms. Trebek to walk around as a moving audience, and part of the class...not walled off from it behind a teacher's desk. it allows a teacher to direct the give-and-take of listening and public speaking. In addition, kids know Ms. Trebek can be looking over their shoulders at any time. What did you do as a student, fearing or looking forward to the appearance of the teacher behind you? Didn't that depend on how well you had been working? It still works.

Another possibility is to arrange the desks in concentric *U's*. This is as good for getting around the room and also helps in class discussion. Kids see more faces, this way, to talk and listen to.

NEVER APOLOGIZE FOR CONTENT.

Content is never boring; teachers and students are. The job is to make content and work engaging. Content must be made interesting, accessible, and exciting without lowering standards or dumbing content down. That is condescending and assumes we think students can't do the work. Behavior is often determined by perception. Do we perceive our students as highly capable rich suburban kids and treat them as such, or do we condescendingly approach them as poor, little ghetto kids who need our help to become what policy makers call "proficient" and treat them as such? *They know what evil lurks in the minds of men....*

What does that do to their self-esteem and our ability to challenge them? We cannot ever think work is too hard for them. We must figure out ways to motivate them to do it. For inspiration, see the movie, *Stand*

and Deliver (1988), about Jaime Escalante at Garfield High School in East Los Angeles. You may know the story.

> In the predominately Chicano area of East Los Angeles, California, in 1982, in an environment that values a quick fix over education and learning, Jaime A. Escalante is a new teacher at Garfield High School in Los Angeles County, California, determined to change the system and challenge the students to a higher level of achievement. Escalante is at first not well liked by students, receiving numerous taunts and threats. As the year progresses, he is able to win over the attention of the students by implementing innovative teaching techniques, using props and humor to illustrate abstract concepts of math and convey the necessity of math in everyday lives. He is able to transform even the most troublesome teens to dedicated students. Escalante realizes that his students have far more potential, so he decides to teach them calculus.

> Despite concerns and skepticism of other teachers, who feel that 'you can't teach logarithms to illiterates,' Escalante nonetheless develops a program in which his students can eventually take AP Calculus by their senior year, which will give them credit toward college. The vast contrast between home life and school life, however, begins to show, as these teens struggle to find the balance between what other adults, and especially their parents, expect of them, and the goals and ambitions they hold for themselves. Several students must confront issues at home. With Escalante to help them, they soon find the courage to separate from society's expectations for failure and rise to the standard to which Escalante had set for them.

> Taking the AP Calculus exam in the spring of their senior year, they find that they have all passed, a feat done by few in the state. Later that summer, the Educational

Testing Service calls into question the validity of their scores when it is discovered that similarities between errors is too high for pure chance. Outraged, Escalante feels that the racial and economic status of the students has caused the ETS to doubt their intelligence. In order to prove their mathematical abilities and worth to the school, to the ETS, and to the nation, the students agree to retake the test at the end of the summer, months after their last class. The students are given only one day to prepare, and Escalante gravely tells them that the test will be harder than the first. The students all pass, and Escalante tells the school principal that he wants his students' original scores reinstated. (http://en.wikipedia.org/wiki/Stand_and_Deliver)

Whether this story is familiar or not, we need to look around. What do we want to do? Do we want to teach toward the "quick fix" of proficiency, or do what Escalante did, and challenge the students to a higher level of achievement? By doing so, he not only got them to achieve superior results on one of the hardest standardized tests high school students may face, he got them to change their self-perception, self-esteem, and behavior.

As much as kids hide that they really want to be challenged, they show how they don't want to be hassled. They are the best at playing the "I can get away with it" game. If they know we will hassle them for not answering, they will answer. If we are clearly not going to settle for any old answer, they will understand the rules of the game and play it our way. If a kid is defiant...we don't get in a shouting match with him; we restate the expectations and provide a reasonable sanction. Nemov (2010) gives this example: "James, you don't have to get the answers right in my class, but you will be expected to try. See me at [lunch, after school, a free period, etc.]."

Why is this important? The culture many kids survive in says to establish oneself as tough but fair, to maintain respect. That includes the teachers in their culture. Teach them that they are accountable for their actions, and are responsible for their learning. Get them to understand that it is ok to help their peers get the answers right. Get them to feel the goodness of success.

CHARACTER, NOT CHARACTERS

Early on in Spike Lee's *Do the Right Thing*, Da Mayor, as played by Ossie Davis, and Mookie, as played by Spike Lee, have this very short exchange. Mookie is hustling down the "ghetto" block in Brooklyn's Bedford-Stuyvesant section, delivering a pizza (his job), and Da Mayor (the block drunkard) is sittin' on a stoop, half hung-over and watching the kids on the block.

Da Mayor: Doctor.

Mookie: C'mon, what? What?

Da Mayor: Always do the right thing.

Mookie: That's it?

Da Mayor: That's it.

Mookie: I got it. I'm gone.

This short exchange is the essence of the movie. It is the essence of life. It is the essence of a teacher's job. Da Mayor is a disrespected elder who, in fact, is the most respectable character in the movie because of how he acts toward others. Mookie is a good kid trying to figure out where he fits in the battle between the two cultures in which he must live. He isn't sure if he wants to be in the mainstream culture, as represented by his sister, or the street culture of "Radio Raheem" and "Buggin Out." It is summertime. We don't know his school behavior, or if he is still in school. We do know he slacks off, but still "just wants to get paid." Mookie is trying to code switch.

Teachers are Da Mayor. Mookie is one of our kids. How do we teach him to "do the right thing"? Da Mayor, ultimately, cannot, because he is a "an old drunk zero." His actions don't match his words. Do ours as teachers, parents, or bosses? Words are only respected if they match actions. We do not want to be known as a, "Do as I say, not as I do" kind. For students to come over to the "right" side, we must model the behavior we expect. Only then, will we develop character, not characters, in our classrooms.

So, even as misbehavior is observed, how can adults respond nonjudgmentally and non-condescendingly? For example, if three kids come in the room too noisily, try "Whoa, have we forgotten how we enter? Let's do that again, and try to do that the way you know how." That works a lot better than screaming, " Moe. Larry. Curly. What the h--- is wrong with you three? Are you incapable of entering correctly?" Even if it was only three kids, no one has "lost face," and there still was an appropriate teaching moment. "Moe, Larry, and Curly" know they were late. By preserving their anonymity, they have moved a step closer to trusting and respecting that adult for not "dissin'" them in public.

As teachers speak, they are judged. Are they to be respected, or not? Are they to be trusted, or not? Are they condescending, or not? Are they encouraging, or not? Verbal, and even (dare I say) physical, pats on the back show belief in students and the desire for them to succeed. Constant, but not nagging, reminders of higher expectations and methods to achieve them signal support and confidence. Challenging them is a sign of respect. It acknowledges their abilities as human beings in our society.

IT'S THE IMPROVEMENT, STUPID

Testing is important. How much better has each student gotten at specific tasks? What is testing actually supposed to test? Improvement. How each student compares with other students is nowhere near as important as how they compare to themselves and where they started in September. Each year in school is a new test. It is amazing how kids of all backgrounds sit up and nod yes, when their new teacher say something as simple as, "We will focus on how much better you are in June than how you are now in September at each of the following. . ." Scores stop being judgmental. They become teaching tools to help students measure their own progress with their teachers' help.

This assessment starts at the very beginning, whether it is the beginning of the year, term, day, or class period. How a teacher begins sets the tone. Most students, even the best "scholars," are still kids who, as Cindy Lauper sang, "just wanna have fun." You don't know what happened to them just prior to coming to your class. They may have been half asleep for a variety of reasons, chillin' with some buddies during lunch, frustrated by a previous teacher, or excited by a great test result. Whatever emotional state they are in as they arrive at the classroom door, they must be immediately tuned to the mindset expected in a class.

Diagnostic tests are also an important tool. The results must be transparent, and acknowledged by students, their parents, and teachers. Everyone must know that these tests will be given again to measure the mastery of specific tasks. Once it is clear that students have "gotten it," new markers are established to push the skill levels to the next plane. At the end of the semester or year, the growth of each student at each task should be clearly seen. When kids clearly see that they can do something they never expected to be able to do, they have experienced success and now understand what it takes to accomplish that feat: high, yet achievable, goals and attention to detail. (By the way, a teacher's success is achieved the same way.)

CHAPTER 6:

"I LOVE IT WHEN A PLAN COMES TOGETHER."

PLANNED "SPONTANEITY"

What would you think of an actor in a play who didn't know her lines? What do you think of an "improv" artist who couldn't improvise? Good teachers are both actors and "improv" artists in every class setting. Isn't improvisation the opposite of planning, you ask? Not exactly. I call it "planned spontaneity." To be accomplished smoothly it takes creativity, flexibility, content knowledge, and an awareness of your students. Ms. Brooks needs to be able to anticipate what she might do if her question isn't clear enough, or if her kids don't get it, or if they go off on a tangent. She has to anticipate the wrong answers and know how to rephrase her questions or try another tact. And, she needs to know when to veer off course and get back on. That can only be done if she planned well.

A lesson is a sentence within a Unit. The Unit is a paragraph within an Essay. And the Essay is the yearlong Curriculum or Syllabus. Ms. Brooks has to understand the whole in order to teach the parts. Only then is she ready to plan what and how to teach. Scrambling from day to day with no clear connections (for kids to understand why it is important to learn *a* before *b* so they can understand *c*), causes kids to scramble. Kids have to learn how to see long-term and make connections between the present, the past, and the future in all subjects, not just history.

Ms. Brooks can not start planning with, "What will I do today?" Today was planned yesterday or earlier. That does not mean that spontaneity is a bad thing. It is wonderful. I can't tell you how often a last-minute, spontaneous idea turned out better than a previously thought out plan. In what profession is spontaneity the master plan?

Nor can Ms. Brooks rely on the activity being the "thing." Teaching is not babysitting or camp counseling. The activity has to fit the goals of the lesson, just as the lesson fits in the unit. More important, and perhaps least discussed, is learning how to prepare quality questions. That is even more important than planning activities.

Lemov says to start with the end. Does he think that is new? Grant Wiggins, long ago, called it backward planning. Longer ago (published in 1941), The New York City Association of Teachers of Social Studies called it "Developmental Planning."

Outcomes: What exactly do teachers want students walking out the door being able to know, think, feel, and more able to do? Those are the goals. How will they be achieved?

Motivation (Hook): This is what invites students to be intrinsically interested in the lesson.

The Aim [not the Do-Now, objectives, or SWBAT (Students Will Be Able To)]: This is an essential question or posed problem that the lesson revolves around. The class should be able to answer or do it by the end of the period. Being able to do it shows the outcomes (goals) have been achieved. Note: *goals* are not synonymous with *objectives*. They are broader. Objectives, as listed under the "SWBAT" format, are skills.

Appropriate material(s): What are the best readings, film clips, activities, etc., to use to achieve the outcome that is manageable based on time. They must be challenging, interesting (fun is good too), and very specific to the task, yet manageable by students in the time allotted.

Participation: This is key, quantitatively, and more significantly, qualitatively. The goal is to get as many kids involved as possible in as many ways as possible, avoiding one-word or short answers whenever possible. Student s have to make talking in full sentences, or even paragraphs a habit.

Questioning technique: Questions (and their **correct** answers) are the real plan. These move the class through the content and materials meaningfully. Questions should strive to get the fullest participation at varying levels. Students have critical-thinking skills. Good questioning allows these to flourish.

Board (Smart, chalk, or white) work: What do we want students to have as notes they can study in the future? What kind of organizational formats do we want them to learn to use? Notes should not be random. Organization must be modeled by using various styles, depending on the goals that day. Harvard-style outline, charts, lists, or other graphic organizers are all choices that can be good (or bad if not matched with the lesson). It doesn't matter if the board is white, black, green, or Smart, if it is not used well.

Conclusion: This can vary. It can range from a simple summary that students do to a more complex application or persuasive exercise. This has two roles. A good conclusion is the lesson's goal and it's assessment. Did students "get it." There are many ways to do this.

Application: Often forgotten, this is key. It connects the lesson to the world of your students. It helps them understand why they have to know or be able to do that.

RHYTHM AND RHYME
"ALL THE WORLD'S A STAGE,

And all the men and women merely players:

They have their exits and their entrances;

And one man in his time plays many parts."

What the Bard left out is that all classrooms are little worlds and that the teacher and students play many parts. The biggest part the teacher plays is director-conductor-choreographer. Students are actors, following the script (ad-libbing is allowed), the music, and the blocking. The pace of the class, it's rhythm, is set by the director. Successfully played, it changes from being slow and deliberate, to fast, furious, and up-tempo, then more moderately paced. The words are a dialogue, led by adroit questioning mixed in with the giving of truths, and the exhilaration of mass participation. The movement is blocked to include upstage and downstage movements, as well as set changes within the room. The result is a class period that, as a production, has a clear first act, a series of continuing acts, and, finally, a climactic act with a definite conclusion.

Similarly, when I teach students how to present a project publicly, whether to a class or an audience, I ask them two central questions. The first question is, who is your audience? So the presenter has to consider who is in the audience and how to reach each group and individual. The second question is, how long is the presentation to be?

Shakespeare knew full well that he had to divide his plays into segments. Acts and scenes were set with varying pace to keep the interest of even his most dispassionate followers. Students need to know that their thirty-minute presentation should really be a series of smaller, clearly connected, interconnected parts following a central thread, yet with a variety of pace, and media.

Sound familiar? It's a class period, of anywhere from 40 minutes to 120-minute blocks. So-called planning "gurus" call for a regimented script. "One size Fits All"? What fun! Nope. I prefer to use another term: a *game plan*. Game plans aren't regimented. They are guides. Each class period, topic, and aim demands a structured approach that follows the game plan, yet is appropriately written, directed, choreographed, and conducted based on the audiences, and that follow good pacing and questioning procedures, without being so robotic that kids can accurately predict what you will do and say next.

Often, these same gurus (a certain Teachers College model comes to mind) will show their own condescending attitudes toward children of certain backgrounds by saying that no activity should be longer than eleven minutes, because that is the length of their attention span. Well, what if it is? Do we want it to stay that way, or is it our obligation to teach them to lengthen it, by actively lengthening it in a controlled situation? Knowing audiences is important here, too. There will be some students who need to be taught how to focus on an activity so they can finish in the allotted time, as well as kids who rush through something just to get it over with.

Every solution to a problem, in turn, creates a new problem with its own new solution. It's the history of mankind. No heat? Create fire. House on fire? Create a fire extinguisher. Can't carry that carcass fast enough or far enough? Create a wheel. Can't stop the wheeled cart before you go over the cliff? Invent brakes. You get the picture. Think kids' attention spans are too short to learn? Create a well-constructed, non-robotic, non-condescending "game" plan that proactively creates appropriate changes of pace, tempo, media, even groupings. This can be done without the sacrifice of answering a central essential question or dealing with a serious theme. It should not be done in little, boxed, eleven-minute activities that simply reinforce the eleven-minute attention span.

A GOOD TEACHER ALWAYS SELF ASSESSES:

- How well did this lesson accomplish the goals on all levels: content understanding, skill development, and appropriate behaviors?

- How well were students engaged today? Were they motivated to do their best and stay on task? Did they walk out of class buzzing (positively) about what they did?

Can the lesson achieve its outcomes in one class period, from motivation to conclusion and application? A good lesson is more circular than linear. The end is connected to the beginning, like a good essay's conclusion reflects its introduction. You must make sure you plan to complete the circle. Too often, teachers over-plan. Novice teachers don't recognize (and experienced ones often forget) that the end of the lesson is equal to, or greater than, the beginning and middle.

Did they get it? A short activity, a few questions that demand brief, yet well-constructed, full-sentence answers, a discussion or debate, or a homework assignment has to be part of the plan to assess your work, as well as theirs. It doesn't need to be quantitative. You are measuring what they learned, for them, not for a superintendent.

Did the goals, outcomes, and objectives guide the choices of activities and questions? Although this seems so obvious, you'd be surprised at how many times this is ignored or forgotten.

Did the lesson lead to student growth? Did it teach students to learn how to learn the processes necessary to live a life as a successful adult? These processes involve not only basic skills, but also communication skills and more complex skills to interpret and appreciate poetry, or analyze and interpret film, or to understand Dr. Martin Luther King's significance to the civil rights movement. The *Aim* (or essential question or problem of the day) frames the outcome. The *objectives* (SWBAT) refer to the skills used to do so. Both are necessary in planning. Both become the foundation for a successful life.

How do students know what's going on at any given time during the lesson? How would any visitor know that? Again, there's a simple answer. An *Aim* or *Problem* at the top of the board (Smart or otherwise) is a "Header." It guides everything and needs to be there for the kids to put in their notes. Yes, I said notes. Imagine doing research without organized notes. Imagine trying to study for a test or assessment a few days or weeks later without organized notes. The fact is most students even in college don't know how. They have to be taught how and why it is important.

It looks like this:

AIM: Why is Martin Luther King still important thirty-four years after his assassination? (*This equates to an essay question to be asked as an assessment.*)

The notes will look like an outline. Harvard-style outlining is fine. The outline is based on carefully prepared questions in a carefully prepared sequence and their expected answers using the preparation and material given students. (*This outline is the outline for that essay asked by the AIM.*)

As a result of working this way students can turn to this page and prepare to answer a similarly worded (but not exactly the same) essay question about Martin Luther King, or questions that ask for more specific, shorter answers, or even (God forbid) multiple-choice questions about Martin Luther King.

Pacing refers to time management. Our Ms. Brooks needs to consider each part of the lesson's length and how to efficiently go from one to the other, so she can complete the circle of the lesson...including the application This includes changing speeds, types of questions, even the activities, in a quick, deliberate fashion, and not getting caught in poor transitions.

WHAT ARISTOTLE KNEW

"It Is the Mark of an Educated Mind To Be Able
To Entertain a Thought Without Accepting It."

Ok, Aristotle wasn't always right, but if it wasn't for this quote, Galileo would have never proven him wrong about objects falling at rates according to their weight. Imagine the spectators at the Tower of Pisa when he dropped a bullet and a cannonball, and they landed simultaneously. He experimented not only with weight, but also with surface area (thus understanding that a piece of paper and another object of the same weight with less surface area fall at different rates, due to the upward force of air.) Enough already with the physics; the key is that Galileo asked a critical essential question of Aristotle's theory. How is the motion of falling objects determined? Now, of course, one question led to a series of interrelated subsidiary questions that needed to be asked in order to answer the *big* essential question. That's how a good plan works. It starts by asking a good essential question, followed by pivotal subsidiary and follow-up questions to lead to a conclusion.

Once again, we arrive at another essence of developing critical teaching skills. This can only be done with good questioning technique. Lemov is correct again when he states (2010, 235) that, "Effective questions tend to come in groups that make the whole greater than the sum of the parts, and questioning is the art of sequencing those questions in groups." Thus, a good lesson plan has an Aim (*the* big, essential question or problem to be solved by the end of the period); a series of written, "Pivotal" (subsidiary how and why) Questions; and a series of unwritten (but planned) detailed and follow-up questions, depending on how students respond to all the other planned, more critical-thinking questions. Too often, the latest reform trends tell us to scaffold questions from low to high and from concrete to abstract. Why? Low expectations.

Let us rather challenge by starting with asking questions like curious kids do (before we teach them how not to be curious). The first thing they ask is, "Why?" You give them the answer. What is their response? Why? "Who is on first? Why? Left field. Naturally." (Oh, I digress.) Why do our well-meaning reformers think kids are not still interested in answering why? What's their next favorite question? How. How does that work? How do you do that? How did they do that? Who, what, when, and where are merely incidental and necessary smaller steps to answering why and how, the questions of curious, critical thinkers.

Thus, the best questions to develop *natural*, critical, thinking skills *naturally* build on our *natural*, childlike curiosity. *Naturally.* Concrete questions are the follow-up questions to fill in the details to understand the bigger why and how. Questions aren't linear. They aren't graduated in their use. Critical-thinking ability depends upon a person's ability to manipulate information to answer questions, rather than being manipulated by scaffolded questions leading to information overload. The distinction between those who can solve a problem and work their way out of a situation is in the ability to ask the right, critical questions to identify the problem, and then ask what it takes to solve it. A linear, concrete series of questions simply gathers information, without regard to how well it answers the bigger question or solves the problem, thus leading to information overload and frustration.

Sentence structure is important in questioning. More harm is done to students from cool teachers asking poor questions than by boring teachers asking good questions. Students have to be taught *why* it is important to analyze questions and *how* to do it, before they will put the energy into defining the concrete, directive terms and content terms necessary to understand *how* to answer any question. All of that is modeled every day by good teachers. If students answer why and how from the very beginning, every day, because teachers expect them to, then we won't have to spend as much time in test prep for those pitifully constructed standardized tests. *Why?* Because you have been doing it every day, *naturally.*

GREAT TEACHERS ASK GREAT QUESTIONS

The typically poorly done class "discussion" looks like this: The teacher asks a "who-what-when-where" question. Student *A* answers. Teacher responds and elaborates, because the student's answer was inadequate. The teacher asks another question. Either student *B* or student *A* answers, and so on and so forth, until the teacher thinks he has finished and done a good job. Well, has he? *No.* Everyone except the teacher and 3 students is now asleep or screwing around. This type of lesson is why education needs to be reformed. The good teachers ask questions that force kids to talk to one another.

Let's suppose that even with good board and notebook notes, good behavior, and lots of smiley faces, we ask this question, How many kids *actively participated* out of thirty? Let's say fifteen. That's half. Is that good? What did the other kids do? How do you know what they know or understand if they were never assessed orally? Let's examine those who spoke. What is more important, that they spoke, or what they actually said? Did they reply in full sentences? Were they simply regurgitating? Were they giving simple, factual answers that exhibited no depth of understanding? If all that is true, then how good was this lesson?

How can the lesson be better? Let's look. Suppose the teacher asked a question that demanded point of view about a fact or situation? Suppose the teacher asked a how or why (pivotal or essential) question to solve a problem. Student *A* answers, and students *B, C, D,* and *E* react and discuss their points of view or add to what student *A* said. Teacher asks a follow-up question about what was said to gain further insights and more detailed elaboration based on evidence.

The teacher says, "Student *F,* what do you think about what student *E* said earlier." "Why didn't you hear her?" "Student *G,* please tell student *F* what student *E* said." During this exchange, the teacher reminds students to look at the speaker, not him, or to look at their audience rather than him. "Don't look at me when you speak. I am not your audience, the rest of the class is." (He continually circulates, making them speak louder and more clearly and in complete sentences. He leaps to the board to note what they said in his planned outline or graphic organizer, modeling and prompting their behavior.) This continues until the lesson is finished.

Let's see. Will the teacher have gotten all to speak? *No.* More than in lesson number one? Probably, because many of the follow-up questions were designed to get kids to easily add or react to what was previously said. More significantly, what did the kids say? They showed understanding, knowledge, and point of view. Perhaps they also added analysis and synthesis. Could the teacher get a better assessment of those skills, as well as content knowledge? *Yes!*

All of that has to be expected behavior, taught early in the year, and continually modeled and reinforced by a powerful leader of students. These are habits good students have, even if their grades don't reflect them. We can't let students give up if they don't grasp these skills as quickly as others. It takes time to get better at everything, learning and teaching included. What's important is that we don't give up on them. We must continually believe in them and in our teachers' abilities to get the best out of them. The type of discussions in classes tells them what we think of them. As we demonstrate our belief in them, they will believe and grow more and more.

Engaged kids feel they are part of the lesson. Group and independent work at a desk or desktop are not the only answers. They are the easy answers. Focused involvement is the proof. Sometimes, however, there are kids who, for a variety of reasons, don't like to do the let's-raise-hands-thing. They have to be volunteered, because they won't. Eye contact indicates readiness. Often, it is a matter of confidence. Special signals can be developed for reluctant speakers to give when they feel they can answer. Once reluctant speakers get past stage one...the opportunity door has opened.

In what is called the Socratic Method, the teacher asks a pivotal (essential) question and becomes the moderator of a class discussion. The first rule, about hands will vary. While first learning how to have an adult conversation, hands are raised, but over time, students should be able to learn how to wait their turn. To start, the teacher may submit their answer for discussion or call on a first student responder. From that point on, the speaker recognizes the next, and the teacher moderates, records their answers and moves the conversation along, using new essential questions or follow-up ones. The other rule is that no one speaks twice until all have spoken once. Simple. Two rules. All other "rules" follow what you have been teaching about conversation and listening.

In 2011, I watched IBM's Watson computer defeat two of Jeopardy's long-time champions simply because of decoding speed. The frustration on the faces on the human contestants said it all. Whatever method of interactive engagement used can't be rushed. Again, it is imperative for teachers to know their kids. Some kids hear, decode the language, analyze the question, compute or find the answer, process it into understandable language, and raise their hands *much* faster than others. The kids who process the question the fastest are often the only participants in a class.

This is the importance of "pause time". Slower processing students must be given an equitable chance to get in the race to the top. If Ms. Brooks asks a student a question, she must know how long it takes him process. Waaaaiiiiiiiit. If he still can't answer, she has to move on and ask another student to help out. In a rush, teachers often step on their students' lines. This ain't Broadway. Teachers have to listen for cues and react accordingly.

Sometimes, the best pause time occurs when students are told to write the answer first. This allows them to plan their answers and provides a written assessment as well. These can be great introductory or summary activities, part of your assessing how well they understand the lesson and how well they can answer the aim of the lesson.

SIMPLE RULES OF QUESTIONING

1. *How* and *why* are the critical-thinking terms. Add to that, "to what extent." "To what extent was the author relating his own opinion?" That asks a student to quantify. It asks how much. Add to that, "so what?" "So what" asks a student to figure out why (or to what extent) something is important or significant.

2. Ask one question at a time. Do not repeat it. Do not rephrase it. Give students *pause time* to think about how to answer it. This is especially true of questions that ask how, why, to what extent, and so what.

3. Try to avoid questions that will result in yes or no answers. What have you gained?

4. Plan. Plan. Plan. Not only have your pivotal questions planned, but also anticipate what your follow-ups (the five *w*'s) might be.

5. Make questions probing, rigorous, and thoughtful, without being wordy. A good question, like a good sentence, is both concise and precise.

6. Never start by asking, Who can...? What does that question answer?

7. Oh no...silence after asking a question. Did they get it? Was it too wordy? Was it imprecise? Break the question down into parts your students can handle, and then build the whole from these parts.

8. Push the envelope. Continually force students to draw conclusions. Don't let them off the hook by finishing the thought yourself. Use follow-up questions to get them to draw conclusions.

CHAPTER 7:

READING IS A VERB

THIS IS HOW WE READ.

Reading is learned both at home and in school. What follows works in both. Student critical thinking must be a process. It starts with analysis of the question. It is followed by a careful analysis of the required material to answer the question. It ends with a synthesis of that material that allows students to draw their own conclusions based on what the question specifically asks and the results of their analysis of the material. None of this is possible without reading. Of course, in our twenty-first century world, we have ventured beyond the written word into the worlds of the web, film, and music. These media require important skills as well. Attention to visual and aural detail is critical for both.

The common thread to improve student use of any medium is close attention to detail. The use of deliberate reading, viewing, and listening, often of short excerpts, coupled with good questioning, will get kids to see, hear, and learn things they never thought they could. In reading, the same is true. We, too, often assume that even our best readers read for detail and understanding. They don't. Too often, they simply read faster with a better vocabulary than our lower-level readers. Watch them read. Watch them read information on a computer screen. They don't read; they scan. They don't even skim read. See how they ride the mouse around the page, instead of keeping their hands off of the mouse and reading the passage from beginning to end. It's scary.

Regardless of their skill level, students need to learn how to read for content and detail. *Reading* is a verb. It is a process that can and must be learned. There are four parts to the reading process. They are:

What's that word? This is the process of deciphering text to identify words. Good readers don't have to ask this.

1. What does that word mean? How many words can the student define and understand? Of the two, understanding is more important than the rote memorization of the definition. Words have nuance. Students need to know how words are used differently in certain situations. Better readers can figure that out.

2. Parlez-vous Anglais? Dependent on vocabulary, this is the automatic ability to read rapidly by grouping words into phrases, and thus understanding expression, meaning, and tone.

3. Got it? All of the above, plus the ability to synthesize, make inferences, and draw conclusions.

There is only one way for students to get better at these skills. They must read. Sometimes, that reading must be in the classroom, guided, and a "close reading" of specific material. Doug Lemov calls it "meaningful reading." He defines it as "accountable, moderately expressive, and highly leveraged" (2010, 254-255). Good teachers know it as "necessary." Accountability is simple. You have to test them, not just a few days later, but as they read. Recently, I observed a few teachers in a New York City middle school doing an exercise to get kids to read in school, because reading coaches know the likelihood of reading at home is nil.

This "100-book Challenge" consists of approximately thirty to forty-five minutes of silent reading in their ELA and humanities classrooms. Each student picks a book or books from what was considered their reading level and "reads." Rarely did any of the teachers hold the kids accountable for the work. There may have been a vague journal entry, but there were no specific questions to assess for the four reading components listed above. In fact, it was hard to tell if the books each student chose were even at their level. Rarely was a student challenged to read a book at a higher level. It is only by challenging them that they will improve. When I discussed the program with the reading coach appointed to the school by the NYCDOE, she responded by saying the purpose of the program was simply to get kids to read more in order to develop the habit of reading. Awards were to be given out for the quantity of books read, not the level of books, nor the development of decoding, vocabulary, fluency, and comprehension skills. These students were not asked to show "the capacity to embed meaning into words...recognition of punctuation...and of key words" (Lemov 2010, 255).

"CLOSE READING"

Good teachers use in-class reading time to probe for the skills mentioned earlier. Everyone in the room becomes accountable for whatever the teacher asks, be it pronunciation, definition, meaning, usage, significance, or nuance of a word or phrase. In addition, too often I have observed classrooms where a class read the same material together, with different students reading different passages aloud, but with not one single pause by the teacher to question and assess. When I asked these teachers why they didn't, they responded that they didn't have enough time. They were being held accountable for holding to a strict timetable for the week and reading a number of pages per week.

"Close reading," the practice of slow, focused reading for understanding, uses a few, common practices to follow, besides constant stopping to measure understanding. One practice entails varying the duration and length of readings. Be unpredictable. When Ms. Brooks says, "Thank you Loretta. Now, pick up where she left off, Lucy," you will know if Lucy was reading or thinking of being in the sky with diamonds. Good teachers keep 'em guessing who is next. Although the duration of reading-aloud time should be varied, the times should all be relatively short. This is important; it allows for frequent analysis of what was read, giving them the practice they need, and also allows for more assessment of more students' abilities. It also keeps the story moving and alive.

And now another word about self-esteem....Correct any error. For example, while reading aloud a passage on college applications, a senior in high school sees *prerequisite* and says, "Percocet." Besides wanting to know why this student has drugs on her mind, the more important issue is whether or not this eighteen-year-old could actually decode *prereq-uisite*, let alone define it and understand the importance of the word to her. Because of time, again, many teachers might just say the word and not even have her repeat it. That doesn't solve the problem. A better technique would be to have her break down the word into syllables for her to learn the process of reading a multisyllabic word, and at the same time, see the root and prefix, to help her understand it. Similarly, students might need to be helped, even in a math or science class, with long *a*'s or soft *c*'s. Rather than worrying about self-esteem now, think about their self-esteem as a college student or at an interview. Help them self-correct, but don't admonish them.

Remember, it is better to be able to understand the meaning and nuance of a word, rather than its definition. One of my pet peeves is the use of flash cards given to students by SAT prep courses costing hundreds of dollars. Most of the time, they simply provide synonyms and perhaps a common usage of a word. Of course, students need to know the basic meaning of a word, but they must also be able to use it and recognize how it is used.

Lemov (2010) uses a great example to illustrate this problem. Would you rather be *mimicked* or *imitated*? Is mimicry the most sincere form of flattery, or is imitation? If a student studied a flashcard of the word *imitation*, and it was defined as *mimicry*, would he be able to understand that a description of me imitating my idol, George Carlin, in class was an act of reverence, not an act of mockery? Teachers must strive to make sure students don't make that kind of "innocent" mistake. It could cost them.

In addition, we might do a better job of suggesting higher-level words to use *in lieu* (as opposed to *instead*) of the words they most commonly use. We must ensure the growth of their vocabulary, not merely the maintenance of one they feel most comfortable with. There is also a lot to be said for some very old school methodologies when it comes to vocabulary building. No, I am not referring to those ubiquitous vocabulary lists that only stressed synonyms as definitions.

PUNTOONING

I (as does Lemov 2010) am referring to having students:

1. Use words in at least three different sentences to demonstrate nuance.

2. Compare and contrast words. *There. Their. They're. Its. It's.* (But only after they have been taught separately.)

3. Learn syntax and parts of speech. How do you use *subvert* as an adjective? *Subversive.* How can *subversive* also be a noun?

4. Greek anyone? Latin? Old English? French? What is a word's root? What is the prefix in *subversive*? What is its root? Its suffix?

5. How about good, old-fashioned contextual clues?

One of my son's favorite books when he was a kid was a book written by Jack Medoff called *Puntoons*. A collection of visual puns, it was a great way for my son and other visual learners to learn new words and phrases. By the time he was six, he had developed his own collection. What a wonderful way for kids of all ages to learn how to use and understand words, with humor. You might even have them act it out, as in a game of charades. These techniques can be done at any age. (jackmedoff.com)

Too often, high school teachers take the fun out of life and learning. Art and music can teach reading as well. Teachers who read short passages *dramatically* help students *feel* the meaning of words. They model how words should be read. They insist that their students read with feeling as well to reinforce the emotion of words. Even math and science textbooks can be livened up this way. We have to loosen up, use our imagination and have fun. Reading this way shows children of all ages the rhythmic flow of words. It shows emphasis, pace, expressiveness, and that how words are read matters in how they make a point. Make it an adventure. Have them *overemPHAsize* key words or phrases for effect and to test their ability to see them. Another take on that is to have them *overPROnounce* parts of speech, punctuation (say *COMMA*), transitional words, verbs, nouns, or anything we want to stress. While we are on the subject of *punk-chew-a-tion* (a Puntoon chance for you all), when kids read aloud, we must make sure they do what the punctuation tells them. (*STOP!*)

It's the culture, stupid. Do not dismiss their cultural baggage. This isn't a contradiction. If you want them to buy into reading and writing, you must let them continue to use their particular vernacular and jargon. They are learning to be bilingual. So are we. For example, reading Tupac's lyrics about young, black male, urban life validates their existence and makes them more motivated to read. It teaches you, too. Teachers need to be bicultural. The same can be done for students whose first language is not English. Then you can teach them to be bilingual. Ask them to rewrite those lyrics or readings as prose for the average white dude.

As previously noted, never *ass-u-me* (another Puntoon chance). Make sure they can identify subjects and objects in sentences. Even our best and brightest student-writers often suffer from what I call "pronounitis"--the overuse of pronouns. If they don't pay attention to pronoun usage while they read, how will they learn to write or speak so they are understood? Who is *he*? Who are *they*? What was the antecedent? How many students know what an *antecedent* is? It's never too soon or too late to learn. The same is true about idiomatic expressions. Reading for comprehension is not a piece of cake. "Cake? What flavor? I love chocolate cake. Please give me chocolate cake. Oh, there is none? WTF? You really meant reading for comprehension isn't easy? I didn't know that." ROFLMAO. Do you know those idioms?

THE IMPACT OF PRIOR KNOWLEDGE

Reading comprehension is very dependent on prior knowledge. It is why many IQ tests are no longer given. What was presumed to be common knowledge wasn't very common to many poor urban or rural kids. As a result, their test scores deemed them less intelligent, when they were really just less knowledgeable. That leads us to our next question. What do they know?

Not much. In all the rush to get students to improve reading and math scores, so-called reformers seem to have forgotten that you need knowledge to have comprehension. As a result, in many elementary and middle schools, time has been taken away from social studies and science to focus more on math, reading, and test prep. However, do we know what they know? Do we know how to use their knowledge to our advantage? Do we obtain books and written material they feel comfortable with and enthusiastic about reading?

Another issue is how homework is used. More often than not, I see it used to do nothing more than to finish work from class, rather than gain knowledge from reading to be used to develop comprehension in class the following day or days, through well-developed lesson plans and authentic assessments that test comprehension skills as well.

So, what used to be done via good lesson planning is now to be done (as Lemov and oh so many other misguided reformers suggest) through "pre-teaching students critical facts" in "ten minutes of teacher-driven background" instead of actually having real social studies classes where students can learn about Nazis and World War II, as they read Anne Frank in their reading (ELA) class. Contrary to what reformers will mislead you with, it worked for years. Having ELA reading texts parallel social studies work in a co-disciplinary or interdisciplinary curriculum might do better than a quick mini-lesson on something as complex as the Nazi regime.

The point is that reading comprehension is important in all classes, even traditional math or science classes. Students need to comprehend basic instructions, content knowledge, information from texts, secondary, and primary sources to become more successful students, not simply test takers. Lemov is right when he says students must be taught how to find focal points. They have to be trained how to find crucial points of reference, key ideas, facts, concepts, and even structural writing or filmmaking tools. They also have to have an idea that they are coming.

For example, when I taught high school seniors about inner-city issues and racial problems through the use of Spike Lee's *Do the Right Thing*, it became important for them to see Lee's use of camera angles, color, and lighting as tools for comprehension of the issues in the film. We need to also teach metaphor and simile the same way we teach vocabulary. It doesn't happen magically. We have to stop and point these tools out each time, until we know our students can find them and use them to develop better comprehension. We also must stop long enough to say, in the next paragraph or next scene, "Look for... the author's use of this metaphor, or the director's use of panning."

This takes time. It means we must follow the "less is more" theory. Read fewer books more successfully. Show films more deliberately. Planning each lesson means including time to continually assess student understanding, by asking pivotal, follow-up vocabulary, and summarizing questions as you go, through a close read or slow show of a text or film.

A major part of improving reading and critical-thinking skills is having students answer, conclude, or give viewpoints using evidence from specific sources. Having them answer, "Show us the sentence that leads you to that answer," or "Quote the author and show us the page and sentence" takes time. Less is indeed more if you do use time more effectively, as well as efficiently.

GOOD READING AND ANALYSIS LEADS TO GOOD WRITING.

Not only does good reading lead to good writing, good writing leads to good reading. Assessments can also become good practice tools. Students must write more often given specific directions. For example, if we want them to summarize, we must be specific about not just what we want summarized, but also how we want it summarized. If not, we will end up with wordy, vague, often copied-and-pasted summaries. They must be shown how to use evidence in order of importance. Taught to find significance by ranking the evidence they will habitually say, "Why did I include that?"

Directed to do things such as, "Write the author's three major points, giving two examples from the text for each," or "Write a fifty-word summary of this specific segment of text," (never a chapter), then they will. Giving that back to them, and then directing them (as Lemov suggests) to narrow it down to twenty words, by eliminating all unnecessary words, or replacing adjectives with strong, action verbs teaches them to write using the active, not the passive voice.

One of the best things I've heard of doing is rather simple. They all text and tweet. Direct them to write the best 140-character sentences for a direct purpose. If it is an English class, let them write a tight, well-written catchphrase for a review of a book or play they read. If it's a social studies class, they can write an obit for a current-events person being studying. There are so many fun and exciting ways to teach good sentence structure.

Finally, we can't fall in to the "Standards" trap. So many teachers say, I don't teach to the test, yet don't realize that they actually do out of habit. If new, inexperienced teachers simply use the same TFA or corporate-created lesson plans, worksheets and questions over and over, they are taught to do just that. I have seen this many times. Because many flustered, new teachers are given to relying on these manufactured (just copy these) planning tactics and strategies, many fail to develop their own plans, for fear of failure in this new data-driven, educational world we live in.

Lemov defers to Nancy Boyles's *Constructing Meaning Through Kid-Friendly Comprehension Strategy Instruction* (2004). (Whew, that was an incomprehensible title. I hope the book reads better.) However, both he and I agree that there are some good questions we need to address. First, "How can teachers identify and help students understand the things that are most worthy of 'notice,' and how can they be systematically identified or modeled?" (Lemov 2010, 299). For the record, that is two questions. Lemov could use some mentoring there. Second, "What kinds of observations can students use to notice in the most productive way?" (Lemov (2010, 302).

The answers to those questions is not that difficult.

- Plan to use the right questions and directions as previously suggested.

- Slow down.

- Be creative.

- Take the proper time to do the right things right.

- Focus on the tasks you want students to be able to do well.

For example, the processes of analyzing evidence and then drawing inferences are difficult for many students (and adults, too, if you haven't noticed). It takes work and time. Teachers have to frequently stop and ask directed questions. They have to ask students to reread and point out specific words or phrases that led them to an inference. For students to be more highly skilled and better learners at any level, teachers have to do more in-depth work, slow down, and reduce broad, curriculum demands. Do three books well, rather than five poorly. Choose case studies in primary and secondary sources to understand social studies concepts and themes, rather than rush to cover factoids in the text. Less is always *more*.

CONCLUSION:

"FUNNY THE WAY IT IS"

THE DEATH AND LIFE OF THE GREAT AMERICAN SCHOOL SYSTEM (RAVITCH 2010).

Diane Ravitch is a well-respected author and education expert. Recently, she wrote this indispensible book for educators and policy makers. In it, she discusses the influence of politics on education policy. She points out the bipartisan appeal of charter schools to Democrats and Republicans alike during the Clinton years. It was a way for both parties to reinvent education, as they had reinvented government (by moving right), and to kill unions and privatize. Media also played a large role in this reinvention of education. According to Ravitch, even liberal magazines like *New Republic* "support competition between schools, charter schools, test-based accountability, performance pay for teachers, NCLB, while being ready to battle the teachers' unions." Again, we see a huge move to the right. *The New York Times, Chicago Tribune,* and the *Washington Post* became anti-Linda Darling Hammond (too cozy with teachers and unions, advocate for teacher professionalism) and pro- Arne Duncan (testing, accountability, choice, anti-teacher union) when it was time to "help," President Obama choose his Education Secretary. All of this movement to the right's version of education, privatization, led to two big questions: Would privatization lead to innovation? or, Would privatization lead to top-down control by private enterprise in the name of reform?

Ravitch feels, and I agree, "The new corporate reformers betray their weak comprehension of education by drawing false analogies between education and business. They think they can fix education by applying the principles of business, organization, management, law, and marketing and by developing a good data-collection system that provides the information necessary to incentivize the workforce – teachers, principals, and students – with appropriate rewards and sanctions" (Ravitch 2010, 11).

Somehow, as a result of this shift in education policy leading to the No Child Left Behind Act, testing became a preoccupation and end unto itself, often replacing curriculum and accountability. What policy makers failed to see and understand--mostly because they never asked the right people--is that tests should be based on the curriculum, not replace it, and that reliance on tests simply dumb-down schools to achieve unrealistic test targets. They failed to see that a well-educated person must be able to leave school with the abilities to solve problems, explain ideas, think, debate, and question. These skills should not simply belong to the privileged that go to the "good" schools, but to all students. Let's not fool ourselves. We know that in this country, when "people" look for schools for their kids, at suburban districts with good schools, they use a skin-color barometer. Or, they send their kids to private schools.

What is Ravitch's solution? It is nothing new. Highly qualified educators, from elementary to graduate school, have been saying this for as long as I can remember. "We must make sure our schools have a strong, coherent, explicit, curriculum that is grounded in the liberal arts and sciences, with plenty of opportunities for children to engage in activities and projects that make learning lively" (Ibid.,13). And we have to properly train teachers to accomplish these goals.

The irony is the loss of freedom and innovation by teachers. Top-down hierarchies prevail in a world more concerned with management and school structure, as opposed to teaching teenagers about history. Why are teachers not asked? Why has the word *union* been substituted for *teachers*? Why have teachers and their representatives been dismissed by politicians and the media as obstacles to reform? Ask any good marketer. They all know you need to do five things to win over the masses: 1. Lie; 2. lie often and repetitively; 3. lie loudly; 4. find a scapegoat to blame everything on; and 5. repeat and repeat and repeat.

So how did we get here? The year was 1983. The Reagan administration released *A Nation at Risk: The Imperative for Educational Reform.* I had been teaching for over a dozen years in the Bronx (with a brief, other-worldly experience in an affluent Connecticut suburb because of the layoffs in 1976). We knew that mediocrity was too often the rule of thumb. We knew that there was often a difference between teaching and union rules. We knew we didn't have enough supplies. We were given 1 ream of paper (500 sheets) to make copies for a month for over 100 kids. We knew our textbooks stunk. We knew we had to rely on our own powers and innovations to succeed. We knew that this report was long overdue. However, we were also worried that it would savage all of us; that it would make teachers into the scapegoats. It did. However, it didn't come close to what NCLB, and what came after, did to us as teachers.

Here's what it did. You compare it to No Child Left behind (NCLB). It started by saying, "The educational foundations of our society are presently being eroded by a rising tide of mediocrity." We agreed. We saw it all around us, as many of us tried to rise above it and keep our kids afloat. We also saw it erroneously take on the issues in high schools more so than the elementary and middle schools. We knew, too, that so many of our kids came into high school with horrible skills and an anti-school attitude that we had to fight hard to change.

The report addressed what the commissioners saw as the fatal flaws in the system: poor curriculum, inadequate graduation requirements, poor teacher preparation, and crappy textbooks. They recommended stronger graduation requirements, higher standards for student conduct and performance. At Stevenson High School, we had developed our own higher standards for curriculum and graduation, as well as having superior department chairs who were (at first) primarily teacher trainers. However, as time progressed, they were promoted to assistant principals, and as a result, became more bureaucrats than trainers. We held our students to higher standards of conduct both in class and in the hallways, but were reprimanded by the NYC BOE and *The New York Times* for "too many suspensions."

The report cited reasons for the problems, such as a steady erosion of the content of the curriculum in many schools and the lowering of expectations. At Stevenson, the opposite was true. We added and created curriculum that far surpassed the mediocre. In fact, New York City was one of the leaders in higher expectations for graduation, for example, exceeding the three years of social studies the report recommended by having three and one-half years of social studies required for graduation. The report stated seven hours in school per day should be required. Our day already did, from 8:00 am to 3:00 pm. Finally, the report "envisioned a public school system that offered a rich, well-balanced, and coherent curriculum, similar to what was available to students in the academic track in successful school districts" (Ravitch 2010, 29). We had that, and sighed a breath of relief.

However, we knew there were too many troubles still to be faced. First and foremost was the issue of new teachers. I had already seen many of our best teachers leave (because of the layoffs, advancement as administrators, and opportunities in better-paying and "safer" districts outside New York City). Their replacements left much to be desired, and our assistant principals, whose jobs had once been primarily teacher trainers, were now too busy pushing paper to properly supervise and train these new people. Many of them soon left as well for greener pastures. The report had also addressed this issue by suggesting higher teacher pay, higher standards for entering the profession, and some kind of peer review to be used for teacher advancement salary, and tenure. (In the late '70s, the NYC BOE eliminated the Board of Examiners that tested each prospective teacher in both pedagogy and subject area.) Those of us who were good at what we did welcomed much of what *A Nation at Risk* said. Unfortunately, we were in the minority. Too many teachers were paranoid and insecure. They were against *A Nation at Risk*, as was the union who felt responsible for them. It is the shame of the union that it usually protected the mediocre at the expense of professionalism. It led to the bad rap the union has today. Unlike *A Nation at Risk*, NCLB, and all it has brought forth, had in mind only one thing: improved basic skills as measured by standardized test scores. We have indeed moved backward. So, when teachers and their spokespeople (unions) fight back, it is improperly misconstrued as more of the same protection of the mediocre.

In the late 1980s, District 2 in New York City was fairly successful in raising reading scores using a method called Balanced Literacy. After being hailed by the new, top-down advocates as the greatest achievement ever, it was found that the district's relatively affluent students had something to do with the success. The dictatorial nature of the program's implementation went unnoticed, except by many of the best teachers. I am not going to discuss the relative merits of any reading program, because Lord knows, each one has its own advocates and data sets. What did go noticed was how easily it could be used in districts all over the country, regardless of its questionable merits.

San Diego became the first major city to institute it fully. Ironically, it came home to New York City when Joel Klein became chancellor and implemented San Diego's top-down, corporate-management scheme. In San Diego, reluctant teachers were disciplined, principals were fired, and a new get-tough policy was instituted. Teachers who spoke out were labeled as being antireform (when, in fact, many had done a great deal to reform education over the years with positive results). If you didn't fit the mold, out you went. It was education *1984-* and *Fahrenheit 451-* style. Teachers and their spokespeople (unions) were made into the bad guys, with much help from the corporate media, fighting only for their own self-interests. District tactics were more about control than education. The powers were gaining control of education and that was that. As Ravitch put it, "This strategy assumes that the central planners know exactly what to do and how to do it" (2010, 53). There was no need for teacher inclusion or buy-in. It was ironically a capitalist system following the structure of a command economy. No one knew or revealed that the model district in New York City hadn't really had that much success with this process.

What also didn't become known was that curriculum was sacrificed so reading could be "taught" for three hours each morning. (Oh wait, 9 am-12 noon is the morning.) Once again, after the fact, there was a study of the program's efficacy. A few key points: First, elementary reading went up. Well, half the day was devoted to it. Math stayed the same. Who knows what happened to other subjects; no one asked. We do know kids learned far less geography, history, and art and had far less time for gym or recess. Are we obese enough as a nation? What about San Diego high schools? Oops. Math and reading scores declined as compared to the rest of California.

The American Institutes for Research (AIR) hired to do the evaluation also concluded that teacher inclusion and "buy-in" was necessary for any successful school reform. In San Diego, the more experienced high school teachers bought in less than younger, elementary school teachers. As long as these devoted professionals were critical of the program, the San Diego school leaders called them obstacles in the way of reform, part of the status quo, and, of course, only out to protect themselves. Media and "reformers" alike picked up this anti-teacher rallying cry nationally.

"FUNNY THE WAY IT IS."

Don't you think that the voices of many of the best teachers were ignored, or worse, chastened by non-teachers? What other profession does that happen in? Law? Medicine? San Diego teachers knew what was good and not good. They weren't included. And, so, it has gone on these many years since District 2 in New York City and San Diego. In San Diego, the superintendent who replaced the dictatorial Alan Bersin, Carl Cohn, in his essay, "Empowering Those at the Bottom Beats Punishing Them from the Top," (*Education Week*, April 25, 2007) wrote, "There are no quick fixes in education. School reform is a slow, steady, labor-intensive process...harnessing the talent of individuals, instead of punishing them for noncompliance with bureaucratic mandates and destroying their initiative." He was clear that, "ground-level solutions, such as high-quality leadership, staff collaboration, committed teachers, and clean and safe environments have the best chance of success." He concluded, "Any genuine school reform is dependent on empowering those at the bottom, not punishing them from the top," and that these solutions cannot be mandated by researchers or the political powers that be.

However, Joel Klein in New York City, Arne Duncan, and Michelle Rhee have become heroes in education reform. Klein was chosen to co-chair the report on *Education Reform and National Security* with Condoleeza Rice. They have taken top-down command, economy-style, education management even further. Your favorite teachers would have fought this top-down, corporate structure and imposed learning tactics tooth and nail. They would have been found to be the enemy. They may have been suspended for insubordination, as allowed in most contracts.

"FUNNY THE WAY IT IS."

New York City public schools were once places the city and its working class were proud of. Many high schools (all were enormous then) were among the best in the nation. Oh, how things have changed. There have been many reasons for these changes. I do not intend to go into them. I will also not get into the charter school debate. There are both good and bad public schools, as well as good and bad charter schools (who often have far better students). Let's just say, "It's complex," When Mr. Bloomberg came into office, he decided to go the way of San Diego. His new chancellor, Joel Klein, whose sole experience in education was the six months he worked as a sixth-grade teacher in Astoria, Queens, visited San Diego and brought back Balanced Literacy and dictatorial management. The DOE mandated the use of two McGraw-Hill math products; math and literacy "coaches" to monitor and enforce the new programs; and, finally, the Teacher's College "workshop model" as the prescribed method of teaching. In fact, when criticized by many education experts about these methodologies, Klein responded with a letter written by none other than the very person at Teachers College who would be in charge of implementing the Teachers College "workshop model." Now, that's chutzpah. I have seen this model and watched as students swallow up new teachers, because it doesn't allow them to teach. It simply asks them to facilitate learning through group and individual work, with all lessons precisely defined and ordered. Teacher's worth? Worthless.

This is the new way. Micromanagement presides over good teaching. Highly centralized, top-down hierarchies (like the old GM) rule the day. New education "managers" with no experience in education earn over six figures, regardless of age, while new starting teacher salaries range from $45,530 (bachelor's degree, no prior teaching experience) to $74,796 (master's degree, eight years teaching experience). Teachers who already have a master's degree, but no teaching experience, will start at $51,425" (NYC DOE "Starting Salaries and Differentials," 2013). Large companies get huge contracts to supply test-prep materials and special curricula for schools. Many of these materials have been found so lacking in quality by teachers, that after being used only once, they are never used again.

History, art, music, science curricula, so important in the education of children, are deep-sixed to allow more time for test prep. Reading and math scores rule the roost. But how successful were these draconian measures? As of July 2010, "After years of soaring test results, the number of city students who can read and do math at grade level plummeted on tougher-to-pass state exams. Only 54 percent of third- through eighth-graders passed state math tests this year, compared with 82 percent the year before, a shocking decline of 28 percentage points. Reading scores dropped 27 points, from 69 percent in the 2008-2009 school year to only 42 percent. The gap in pass rates between black and white students in math doubled to 34 percentage points from 17 last year. On the reading exams, the difference widened to 32 percentage points from 22" (*New York Daily News*, July 29, 2010).

> Why? 'What has changed is we are setting the bar higher,' said state Regents Chancellor Merryl Tisch. 'We are finally providing a clear and honest answer to the public to the question, 'How are our children really doing?' 'This year, the state raised the passing score for the exams and made the math test less predictable and added more material. The result was a stunning drop in how many city students are proficient in math and English. Next year, officials say, the exams will get even tougher. Testing experts said that students were able to get the same score by answering fewer questions correctly.' 'There have been problems scaling the tests since 2006,' said former city testing chief and NYU professor Robert Tobias. '[Schools] were duped into thinking they were making these incredible gains and that kids were learning more and more, when in reality they were not.' (*New York Daily News*, July 29, 2010)

If schools didn't improve scores, they were closed. Period. No questions asked. Oddly enough, according to Diane Ravitch, "half of the city's worst- performing schools on the state math tests in 2009 were new schools that had been opened to replace failing schools" (Ravitch 2010, 79). Almost all of this is happening in K-12.

"FUNNY THE WAY IT IS."

On the high school level, the new approach has been equally "interesting." The new DOE fell in love with the idea of small high schools replacing big ones. Of course, large high schools present large problems. But, New York City high schools have always been large. Many were still very successful. However, instead of taking an approach to improve the culture and teaching of these schools, they were uniformly closed. For the sake of smaller learning cultures, instead of breaking these schools into learning academies under one roof and one administration, they were divided into as many as seven different schools with seven different administrative teams. Who gets paid more? Teachers or administrators?

"FUNNY THE WAY IT IS."

Where once stood 100 proud, public, neighborhood high schools, now stand over 425 of various sizes, shapes, and theoretically, themes. Many kids travel hours a day to get to school. Do they do work in transit? How much sleep does a seventeen-year-old get who has to be at school at 8:00 am and must travel an hour each way by bus? For whom was this done? Who decided? The new, small high schools were openly suggested and funded by hundreds of millions of dollars by Bill and Melinda Gates, Carnegie Foundation, and Open Institute Money (Ravitch 2010, 82). The older, larger schools, as did the non-charter K-12 schools, suffered from an open-door policy. As public high schools, they have to admit everyone. The new, smaller (some charter) schools didn't. They still don't. They could admit fewer special-needs children and English language learners. They could "terminate" students who destroyed the school culture. Where did those students go? To the big old schools. So, needless to say, the larger schools kept failing. Little or no money poured into them, relative to the new schools. They continued to struggle, justifying continuing the DOE's policy of closing large schools. If they had tried, they would have found many examples around the country of successful large schools: Midwood High School (3,700 students) in Brooklyn and Brockton High School in Brockton, Massachusetts (4,400 students) are among them. The staffs there do an excellent job doing what large New York City public schools used to do. Teach. There are several studies that show common practices. Why does the NYCDOE ignore them? Could it be the money?

In the fall of 2010, after all of that, the NYCDOE is deciding whether or not to publish "value added" teacher data reports as Los Angeles did at the end of August 2010. Maybe they didn't read the article from *The Los Angeles Times* on September 27, 2010 that said:

> A teacher whose body was found underneath a bridge in the Angeles National Forest appears to have committed suicide.... The body of Rigoberto Ruelas was found Sunday morning around the Big Tujunga Canyon area in the Angeles National Forest, according to the Los Angeles County Sheriff's Department.
>
> Ruelas's death stunned students and teachers at Miramonte Elementary School in South L.A., where he was described as a popular and energetic teacher....'You were an example for each one of your students and a friend for all,' a hand-painted banner said in Spanish. 'R.I.P. Mr. Ruelas.'
>
> KABC-TV Channel 7 quoted family members as saying that Ruelas was distraught about scoring low in a teacher-rating database recently made public by *The [LA] Times*. He had been missing since September 22. South Gate Police Officer Tony Mendez told KCAL-TV Channel 9 that Ruelas was unhappy at his database ranking. In the database, Ruelas is listed as 'less effective than average overall.' He rated 'less effective' in math and 'average' in English.

What an incredible tragedy. Mr. Ruelas's reaction was, of course, extreme, but how would anyone react to that kind of public scrutiny? Why is it that teachers, of all people, can be treated to that type of public humiliation? What is interesting is the comment made by Los Angeles School Chief Ramon C. Cortines after Mr. Ruelas's death. He said, "Mr. Ruelas was a passionate and caring teacher, who put his students first. He made a difference in the lives of so many in his classroom, and by staying after the bell rang to tutor students."

Not good enough to get a decent rating, I guess.

"FUNNY THE WAY IT IS."

Martha Foote, a parent representative of the Testing Task Force in PS 321 Brooklyn, recently published a document entitled "Teacher Evaluations – A Parent's Guide" about these TDRs. Here are some of the findings:

- The DOE's "value-added" model to calculate teacher ratings is unreliable. In fact, a recent study by Sean Corcoran of NYU demonstrates that the New York City TDRs have an average margin of error of 34-61 percentage points out of 100.

- Principals across the city report that many of their best teachers have received poor ratings on their TDRs due to flaws in the model.

- The DOE has used unverified and erroneous raw data to calculate TDRs. In one school, the principal discovered that there were data errors for 3 of the 13 teachers (23 percent) who received a rating.

- The DOE has used flawed test data to calculate TDRs. Specifically, the New York State Education Department declared this summer that the state tests have become easier to pass over the past several years and the test scores have therefore inaccurately represented children's achievement. Yet, these inaccurate test scores are the basis of the TDRs.

- Our children will lose excellent teachers if the TDRs are publicly released. Principals report that some of their best teachers have declared their intent to leave the profession rather than face the public humiliation of a bad rating. (Ask yourself--would you want an incomplete and flawed rating of your job performance to be printed in the local newspapers?)

- Since teachers with seniority have the right to be placed in one of their three top grade choices, it is very likely that experienced teachers will not choose to teach fourth or fifth grade, since these are the only two grades in elementary school where teachers receive TDRs. The result would be that the least experienced teachers would be teaching these grades.

- The public release of the TDRs will promote even more teaching to the state tests. A more critically thinking curriculum, including a focus on art, science, and social studies, will be sacrificed in many schools.

- These actions are an open invitation to scapegoat individual teachers and the teaching profession as a whole, making it less likely that highly qualified college graduates will see teaching in New York City public schools as an attractive option.

- The School Progress Reports that give schools grades of A-F use the same basic value-added approach of the TRDs. Yet, they have fluctuated wildly from year to year, with schools going, for example, from C to A to C in three years, without any significant changes in the school's instructional program or effectiveness. Knowing how arbitrary and often inaccurate these ratings have been for schools overall (where there is actually a larger pool of data than for any one teacher), it is misguided to use these same flawed measures to publicly rank teachers.

- Focusing on this flawed data deflects attention from the deep-seated problems facing our schools, e.g., lack of appropriate funding and support structures, overcrowding, and high-stakes, testing policies.

Apparently, what happened in San Diego and Los Angeles and even here in New York City over the past decade doesn't count. In 2010, there was a debate over Joel Klein's replacement. Mayor Bloomberg, once again, decided that the leader of the nation's largest school system must be someone who is a business manager. "It just goes to show they have no understanding of what the job is," Bloomberg said. He defended [Cathie] Black as a "super manager, magnificently qualified to run an organization with 130,000 employees and a $23 billion budget." Oh well, apparently hizzoner hasn't noted which state has been most successful in reforming schools. Black lasted 3 months.

According to Sol Stern, in *The City Journal* (November 16, 2010), "In sharp contrast to Bloomberg's New York, Massachusetts has been the nation's leading exemplar of what I have called the "instructionist" approach to education reform. Starting in the mid-1990s, a coalition of reformers pushed the state's board of education to mandate rigorous curricula for all grades and created demanding tests linked to those curriculum standards. Guess which school system has produced greater and more meaningful academic achievement gains on the unimpeachable, national NAEP tests?"

The most successful districts are not that way simply because they have the "best" students. They draw and hire the best *teachers*. These districts have common characteristics: supportive administrations, mentor-teacher programs, intervisitation, collaboration, academic freedom, higher pay with good benefits, even sabbaticals for study (and may I say again, mentoring by master teachers and supervisors in their areas of study).

Furthermore, let's cut to the chase. Even the best districts must replenish and add to their teacher corps. They rely on newer, younger teachers regularly to replace the master teachers who retire (to write?). The fact is that most new teachers aren't well trained enough, especially with so many coming out of TFA "basic training" and having the Teacher's College "workshop model" being thrust upon them. Pam Allyn, Executive Director of LitLife, put her finger on the most important issue in a letter she wrote to *The Journal News* on November 14, 2010:, "All of us remember our best teacher[s]. If you ask yourself which teacher changed your life, you can readily name that teacher without any hesitation." It really is that simple.

The characteristics and methods of those teachers must be passed forward to new hires. Who best to do that but the masters themselves? This bears repeating. New teachers need better training from wherever they are from, be it TFA or universities. Too often, they have courses in pedagogy taught by poor teachers. How does that work? Poorly. New teachers should be actively supervised by highly qualified mentors during an internship period, as are doctors. This must be on site and regular. It cannot be once in a blue moon, monthly, or quarterly.

Finally, whether given a sabbatical or not, teachers need reinvigoration and to keep abreast in their field. The best districts also offer in-service courses or access to local universities to upgrade their teachers' skills and knowledge. Massive overhauls of schools are not necessary, even in huge urban districts, if these steps are taken. Teacher ratings are not necessary. The hundreds of millions of Bill Gates's and other foundations' money would be better spent on making sure districts followed these simple and proven actions, rather than top- down, micromanagement by non-educators.

WHY REFORMERS ARE LIKE REPUBLICANS

Okay, I know education reformers come from all political backgrounds. However, the ones who get the most publicity have learned a few things from successful Republican Party campaign tactics. "If there is one thing that can be done for the country, one thing, improving education rises so far above everything else." Good God. Who wouldn't agree with that? The problem is that quotes like these in the hands of reformers or their media hacks are often used to say that anyone who disagrees with their form of reform is antieducation and therefore anti-American. Such is the case with this quote of Bill Gates by Jonathan Alter in *Newsweek* (December 6, 2010, p 20). Our economic destiny is at stake, Alter concludes, because of the fall in international education ratings. The culprit? Seniority. The Villain? Seniority.

Alter, mimicking Gates, seems to believe that the seniority system is the root cause of all of our education troubles. It is "the two headed monster–it is expensive and harmful." He points out that perhaps Gates was wrong in his earlier push to rid education of another villain, large schools, but vindicates him on the basis of "at least he is trying." That sounds an awful lot like social promotion for billionaires. Anyone who goes against Gates, like Diane Ravitch, is fair game for attack. He quotes the man behind the Microsoft monopoly and its "blemishless" history of software failures as saying, "Does she [Diane Ravitch] like the status Quo? Is she [Diane Ravitch] sticking up for decline?" Because he [Bill Gates] says so, she must be. Alter, not to be outdone, concludes, "There's a backlash against the rich taking on school reform as a cause. Some liberals [oh oh, here we go...scapegoat time] figure they must have an angle and are scapegoating teachers. But most of the wealthy people underwriting this long- delayed, social movement for better performance are on the right track. Like the rest of us, they know that if we don't fix education, we can kiss our future goodbye."

Who wouldn't agree with that statement? The problem is the faulty logic. Based on Alter's theory, the only way to fix education is how Gates and the other rich corporate leaders want it fixed. If *A* (corporate education reform) then *B* (education success) then *C* (international improvement and economic security). This is syllogistic reasoning. Let's go back a bit. Is seniority a problem? Yes. Are entrenched, mediocre minds in education a problem? Yes. Is Gates's solution the answer? That is Alter's logic. Why? As the old radio commercial went, "Money talks. Nobody walks." Nonsense.

To reiterate. Teachers must have due process. I have never been a fan of seniority. I saw its flaws as a gifted, young teacher laid off because I lacked it, while hacks kept their jobs. I almost came to blows with a colleague who introduced himself to me as the "Dave with Seniority" when I was hired back after the nasty layoffs in New York City in the mid-70s. He was a hack, and we both knew it. However, I do know why due process is important on any job. I have seen nontenured teachers laid off for no reason, other than sticking up for educational reform they believed in that subsequently was accomplished after a districtwide effort led by tenured teachers and union leaders. How is that justifiable? Why is it anti-education or anti-American to believe in due process, as in the Fourteenth Amendment? Search me? Oh wait, that might be an open invitation to invasion of privacy.

Historically, how many times have we seen the rich and powerful "my way is the only way" mantra? Usually in feudal societies, monarchies, or dictatorships, where either you are with us or against us. And we know what happens to those who are "against us." Is that how we want our educational reform to perform? No.

The Constitutional Convention is a model we should examine. Representatives from thirteen states met in Philadelphia with different ideas of reforming the America of 1787. Hostility was rampant. Oppositional ideas ran amok. Intense hatreds filled the air. What did they do? They created our Constitution, what many believe is the greatest and most successful compromise in the history of human society, during a time far more trying than ours. Surely, we can do the same in reforming education. Surely, those in education can follow their lead. Leave the lawyers, politicians, media hacks, and corporate heads out of it, and let us figure out how to reform education, so we don't "kiss our future goodbye."

WORKS CITED

Carmichael, Evan. "Motivating-People-at-Work--The-Power-of-Intrinsic-Motivation." www.evancarmichael.com. (accessed February 22, 2010).

Engel, Susan. *Scientifically Tested Tests.*

http://www.nytimes.com/2010/09/20/opinion/20engel.html?_r=0

Gurian, Michael, and Stevens, Kathy. *The Minds of Boys: Saving Our Sons From Falling Behind in School and Life.* San Francisco, CA: Jossey-Bass, 2005.

James, Abigail Norfleet. *Teaching the Male Brain: How Boys Think, Feel, and Learn in School.* Thousand Oaks, CA: Corwin Press, 2007.

Kovacs, Phillip. "Living in Dialogue - Education Week Teacher." *Education Week*: Blogs. http://blogs.edweek.org/teachers/living-in-dialogue (accessed February 7, 2013).

Lemov, Doug. *Teach Like a Champion: 49 Techniques that Put Students on the Path to College.* San Francisco: Jossey-Bass, 2010.

Lepper, Mark R., Greene, David, and Nisbett, Richard E. "Undermining children's intrinsic interest with extrinsic reward: A test of the 'overjustification' hypothesis." *Journal of Personality and Social Psychology* Vol 28(1) (1973): 129-137.

Machiavelli, Niccolo and Donno, Daniel John. *The Prince and Selected Discourses.* New York: Bantam Books, 1966.

Neu, Terry W., and Rich Weinfeld. *Helping Boys Succeed in School: a Practical Guide for Parents and Teachers.* Waco, TX: Prufrock Press, 2007.

New York City Department of Education. http://schools.nyc.gov (accessed February 7, 2013).

New York Times, "Scientifically Tested Tests," September 19, 2010. http://www.nytimes.com/2010/09/20/opinion/20engel.html?_r=0 (accessed September 19, 2010).

Pink, Daniel H. *Drive: The Surprising Truth About What Motivates Us*. New York, NY: Riverhead Books, 2009.

Ravitch, Diane. *The Death and Life of the Great American School System: How Testing and Choice Are Undermining Education*. New York: Basic Books, 2010.

Rees, Jonathan. "Frederick Taylor in the Classroom: Standardized Testing and Scientific Management Radical Pedagogy." *Radical Pedagogy* 3:2 (2001). http:// www.radicalpedagogy.org /Radical_Pedagogy/Frederick_Taylor_in_the_

Classroom__Standardized_Testing_And_Scientific_ Management.html (accessed April 12, 2010).

Richmond, Emily. *Teacher Job Satisfaction Hits 25-year Low*.

http://www.theatlantic.com/national/archive/2013/02/ teacher-job-satisfaction-hits-25-year-low/273383/

Sahlberg, Pasi, and Hargreaves, Andy. *Finnish Lessons: What Can the World Learn From Educational Change in Finland?* New York: Teachers College Press, 2011.

Schwartz, Barry, and Sharpe, Kenneth. *Practical Wisdom: The Right Way to Do the Right Thing*. New York: Riverhead Books, 2010.

Sun, Tzu. *The Art of War*. London: Oxford University Press, 1971.

Teach For America.

(https://www.teachforamerica.org/our-organization/our-history)

Tuchman, Barbara Wertheim. *The March of Folly: From Troy to Vietnam*. New York: Knopf, 1984.

Tyre, Peg. *The Trouble with Boys: A Surprising Report Card on Our Sons, Their Problems at School, and What Parents and Educators Must Do* [Paperback]. New York:

Three Rivers Press, 2008.

Vasquez, Heilig, J., Cole, H. and Springel, M. "Alternative Certification and Teach For America: The Search for High-Quality Teachers." *Kansas Journal of Law and Public Policy* 20(3), (2011): 388-412.

Wiggins, Grant. "The Case for Authentic Assessment." *Practical Assessment, Research and Evaluation*, 2[2] (1990): 100-101.

CPSIA information can be obtained
at www.ICGtesting.com
Printed in the USA
FFOW02n1206011014
7696FF